The Ta... 'Sisters growing up
i... na Fork Valley
in the early 1900's

By

Mary D... Martha Downey W... ian

For The Gordon
Cooper Library

Martha Downer Waterman

Mary Downer Evans

Copyright © 2000 by Mary Downer Evans & Martha Downer Waterman

Gran Farnum Printing and Publishing, Inc.
3401 Grand Avenue
Glenwood Springs, Colorado 81601
(970) 945-9605

ISBN 0 9649593-6-4

Manufactured and printed in the United States of America

We dedicate this book
to our mother, Faith McNeil.
Thank you for your love
and strength.

ACKNOWLEDGMENTS

We would like to thank family members for their encouragement and support with this book. Special thanks go to our daughters, Judy Waterman Huston and Sydney Evans Rupar: also to Mary's granddaughters, Natalie Rupar Davies and Denise Rupar Shives. We couldn't have done it without them. If there are any discrepancies in the text, we are sorry but that's the way two octogenarians remember it.

TABLE OF CONTENTS

DOWNER FAMILY TREE

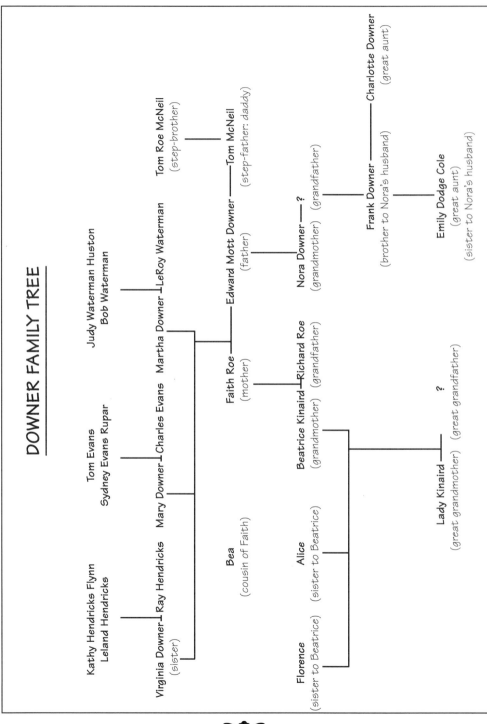

PROLOGUE

Mary: Christmas Holidays 1989, the Rupars were in Colorado so Charles and I had as many of the family as could get together come to Battlement Mesa for a dinner. Judy brought old home movies and since they were silent movies, Sis and I kept filling in the details about what was happening and many things in addition. After we'd seen quite a few of the movies that everyone was really enjoying, Judy and Sydney both said, "Why don't you write down some of those old happenings because we'll never remember all of this." Since we much prefer to talk than to write, we made audio tapes of our family history. Those tape recordings are the text of this book.

REMINISCENCES BY
TWO OCTOGENARIANS

DIALOGUE

Martha: In 1887 our mother, Faith Roe , was born in Binghamton, New York. Her father, Richard Roe, was a newspaper editor. She didn't remember much of him since he died when she was very young. Faith and her mother moved to Columbus, Ohio and lived with her mother's sister, Alice, and Alice's daughter, Bea. Mother grew up in a family of females since her grandmother, Lady Kinaird, came to live with them also.

  While in Columbus, Mom's mother, Beatrice, studied nursing and after she graduated she and Mom moved to Newark, Ohio where Beatrice became nurse to an elderly patient named Eli Hull. Mom and her mother moved into his beautiful home and later Beatrice married Eli Hull.

  Our mother would spend summers vacationing in Granville, Ohio. It was in Granville where she met Frank O'Bannon whose father had one of the first autos in the town. It was a Pierce Arrow. When he started courting Mom he took her driving in it. About this time, our father, Edward Mott Downer, came to Ohio for a visit. He was born in Salina, Kansas in 1886. He had just graduated from St.Johns Military Academy. They fell in love and Mom gave up Frank

Frank O'Bannon and Faith Roe about 1909.

12

Edward Mott Downer graduate of St. John's Military Academy

and his father's Pierce Arrow to marry our father on June 10, 1910 and go west. They went to Pueblo which, at the time, was quite primitive in Mom's estimation. There were dirt streets, few sidewalks and lots of dust. Mom found it very difficult to keep her long white

dresses and petticoats clean. She had to scrub her clothes by hand with a wash board and tub using a strong lye soap. The wash water was muddy and had to be settled the night before any washing was done.

Faith and Ed just married June 10, 1910

Mary: During the years Mom was married to our father we lived either in Pueblo or Leadville. Our grandmother, Nora Downer, had houses in both places where our family could live rent free. Our father was a CPA and we would live in the town which provided the most work for an accountant at the time.

Faith Downer (Right) Early days in Pueblo, Colorado

Martha: Let's remember to tell something about how Mom was raised because it has a lot to do with things that happened later on. And so I think we'll try to recall some of the things that Mom told us about her childhood and about her grandmother and this and that.

Mary: Well, she and her mother lived with her cousin, Bea, and her Aunt Alice. The two mothers and the two young girls.

Martha: and then later their...

Mary: grandmother, our great grandmother.

Eli Hull, Newark, Ohio. Faith's stepfather.

Martha: Yes, the grandmother, Lady Kinaird, came from England to live with them. Lady Kinaird was an aristocrat and the family treated her like royalty. Mom said she never remembered her doing anything except getting up sort of late in the morning and sitting in her chair. Her meals were brought to her. She was waited on hand and foot. Mom said that her grandmother had beautiful hair and she brushed it about five hundred times a day and she prayed on

Eli Hull's home in Newark, Ohio.

her knees for an hour every day (Mary: I didn't remember that) Another thing she told about was that the grandmother didn't like to have people use slang. And mom and her cousin used to say....for YES they would say Uh huh and Huh uh for no...and one day the grandmother said, "I CAN NOT tell the difference between Huh huh and Huh huh" Those are some of the things I remember.

Mary: Back to when Mom was first married, our mother and our father, Edward Downer, moved from Pueblo to Leadville where his mother, Nora Downer, lived. At that time there were no children but not long after that Martha Emily Downer was born in 1912. And some of the first things she remembers are ....

Martha: Well, one of the things I remember is ..... it was before Mary was born so I was probably around two. There were lots of tramps who came by our house. Leadville was a railroad town and there were lots of tramps. They were just men who were out of work and needed something to do. Mom was always a great one to let them cut some wood or something and then feed them. So one morning she had set the table and I was to eat with the tramp. She was going to have the two of us go ahead and eat since it was my meal time. And so everything was on the table and I just sat. Finally mom asked me why I didn't eat and I said, "Well, you didn't say the grace!" And so she had to say the grace for me and the tramp.

Then another thing I remember is when Mary was born....it was the greatest event that could be and....

Mary: That was back in Pueblo.

Martha: Oh yes. We had gone back to Pueblo then.

Mary: Yes, because I was born in 1914 and I was born in Pueblo.

Martha: Yes, so we were back in Pueblo then. Well, anyway, I do remember that our father, who was very strict about certain things, said I was to call my little

Faith and Martha Downer, Leadville, Colorado 1912.

sister by her full name, Mary Elizabeth. So that was fine. So when anybody would come to the house, before they would even get in the door, I would say, "Come and see my little sister, Mary Elizabeth!" That's one of my first memories.

Mary: Going back to the morning that I was born, it was very cold weather. I was born December 21st. The water pipes had frozen and burst during the night and the floor was covered with water. My father must have been a busy man that morning, getting fires going in the stoves, mopping the floors, running to the neighbor's to

Mary Downer about one month old in 1915.

get water to boil and taking care of Sis. Knowing Mom, she was so organized, I'm sure she already had a stack of clean linens ready for my birth.

In those days you didn't go to a hospital, the doctor and the midwife came to the home. It was quite a commotion that morning, but, luckily, I waited until everything was ready before I made my grand entrance.

Martha: And then, I remember, we moved back to Leadville and Mom was very concerned because Mary didn't seem to grow. She was as lively as a cricket but she just didn't grow. But when spring came and Mary could get out...we could get out and play in the yard and Mary could eat the chinking out from between the logs and eat the coal then she began to grow great. That seemed to be her thing.

Another thing in Leadville that was kind of interesting that we should remember is...we lived right across from a whole string of houses owned by our grandmother Nora and that was a red light district. The ladies used to sit out in the windows upstairs and they would visit with us and we thought they were so pretty and nice.

Mary: Our father, Edward Downer, became a compulsive gambler and sometimes there wasn't any food in the house. At one time our mother went down and stayed right at the gambling joint and insisted on seeing the manager. He just let her sit there for a long

Outing to Turquoise Lake when we lived in Leadville.
Grandmother Downer, Mom, Mary & Martha

time. Finally she saw him and made him give back the paycheck that our father had used for gambling so that we would have food in the house. At this time, our younger sister, Virginia, was on the way and Mom was having a lot of problems because our father's behavior became very erratic. He began to disappear for long periods of time. We had no idea where he was. He was no longer able to keep a job and he was providing no support to the family. On one occasion, when he returned home after a long absence, he became violent. Mom, who was pregnant with Virginia at the time, was sitting in the rocking chair with me on her lap. Ed threatened to push us down the stairs, rocking chair and all. He almost did it too!

Mom, Father, Mary & Martha

That was the last straw! Mother left our father and we moved into Grandmother Nora's boarding house. Subsequently Mom filed for divorce. That was in 1917.

Now our mother had to manage to support the family. One of the things she did to help make a living was get a job as pastry cook for the doctors and nurses at a big hospital in Leadville. Our family had always loved her delicious pies with flaky crusts. Now she made pies by the dozens because they were so popular with the hospital staff. That job lasted for quite a while.

Faith and Virginia Downer born June 22, 1917 in Leadville, Colorado.

Another interesting thing she did was raise rabbits. That was in Leadville too. She had no previous experience raising animals of any kind. The first thing she learned (the hard way) was that she should have separated the buck and the pregnant doe before the baby rabbits were born because the buck killed all of the first litter. When Mom managed to raise some rabbits old enough to butcher, she had to summon up a lot of courage to kill those rabbits. She also had to learn to skin them and dress them ready for the store. Raising rabbits was a big undertaking for Mom but luckily it turned out to be profitable.

Martha: Yes, one time, Mary, remember? One of the rabbits...she had a big black buck and it died and we buried it. Believe it or not, the next morning, right on the grave, there was a BIG WHITE BUCK! Now we don't know what happened but that's true, according to Mom.

Mary: Another job that she had was working for our grandmother, Nora Downer, at her boarding house and it was at this boarding house where she met Tom McNeil, a railroad engineer on the

Midland Railroad. He was 35 years older than Mom who at that time was 31. They became very interested in each other and she married him. At that time he retired and had chosen to move to Basalt, Colorado because of the very nice climate. Virginia had been born in June of that year, the 22nd in 1917 and Martha had started first grade and had gone about a half a year of school when we moved to Basalt by train. We had a stopover in Glenwood and had a sip of the sulphur water.

Martha: Oh, one thing I remember is...Daddy told us that the water was hot enough to boil an egg and we thought that was really something!

Mary: When we got to Basalt, it was the year of the 1918 flu epidemic and Daddy wouldn't allow Sis to go to school. In fact, we weren't allowed out of the yard. In Basalt, there was no doctor so Daddy helped take care of the sick. He kept a pair of coveralls just hanging on the back porch. When he went out of the house he would put on those coveralls. He took

Faith and Tommy McNeil Basalt, Colorado 1919.

food to people who were in need and when he came back in he would hang up his coveralls and go right to the boiler that was kept on the stove all the time and boil the dishes that were used by the flu victims he was helping. We got through 1918 fine with none of us getting the flu but in 1919 Mom and I both got the flu, not as badly as the people the year before, but I was sick enough that my nose bled and my ears bled. That was the year that Tom was born. His birthday was February 23, 1919. Later in that year we had an epidemic of whooping cough. Tom and Virginia were both little. Daddy and Mom would grab them by the heels and hold them upside down so they'd get rid of the phlegm but Sis and I had to take care of ourselves. We'd just grab onto a chair until we were exhausted from coughing.

Martha: While we're talking about the things that happened to us, there used to be quite a few epidemics and, at one point, the measles came to town. Mary and I had the measles first and we weren't very sick. Then when Virginia got them Mom was a little worried about her, she was a little sicker than we had been but Daddy said, "Oh, no problem, just put her in a dark room and she'll be fine." (Back then it was thought that measles cause blindness so people would put the patient in a dark room). Then Tom got the measles and Daddy was really upset. This was the first time that Daddy showed any preference for Tom over his step girls. Tom was no sicker than Virginia had been but, to Daddy, he was a SICK BOY.

Although we didn't have very much money we always had a big garden and Daddy used to....

Mary: But Mom always said we would never be broke because she always kept one penny in the sewing machine drawer and no one ever touched that!

Martha: That's right! O.K. So... Daddy used to go hunting and fishing, sometimes out of season. One time he got a deer out of season. My parents referred to the illegal venison as jackrabbit. I was in first grade and I went to school and told the teacher that we had FRIED JACKRABBIT HEART for breakfast. I'm sure she looked kind of surprised.

Mary: Our Daddy and two other men were going to go up to Kelly Lake fishing. (Kelly Lake is on Basalt Mountain about 3 miles north of Basalt). It was early in the spring. There was a lot of snow still on the ground. They went on horseback. They had no sooner left the house than we decided we would follow along behind. It was just

Sis and I. Every once in a while he'd see us and he'd motion for us to go back. We would pretend to go back and as soon as they were around the curve we would start out again. Finally it became pretty cold and our hands were freezing and our feet were freezing and Sis wanted to lay down in the snow and rest. I said, "No you can't do that. You're apt to freeze to death if you go to sleep in the snow". We plunged on and on and finally the men were coming back from their fishing trip. Our feet were soaking wet. We had sat down by the creek and we were dumping the water out of our galoshes when the men came on down. They just went by us like they didn't see us. We felt pretty depressed. They went clear down around the curve before Daddy came back to get us. We were pretty happy to be able to get on that horse to go on back home.

Martha: And then when we got home, do you remember what he did? He made HOT doughnuts.

Mary: Daddy said if we wanted to go to Kelly Lake that bad, we would just plan for the whole family to go for a week. At that time we had a horse named Daisy and we had a two-wheeled cart which would carry quite an amount of supplies. We packed all up and went to Kelly Lake for the week. Up there, there were some old log cabins. There were beds in there that had just springs. The cabins were full of rats so Daddy would have us round up the rats, chase them out and he'd stand by the door and bang them over the head. We stayed at the cabin long enough that we were short of food, about all we had left was oatmeal. Daddy had always insisted that we eat oatmeal for breakfast 365 days a year. He said, "Oatmeal is good for you!" Therefore, we had become SICK AND TIRED of oatmeal. But, in order to stay longer at the cabin we said, "Oh, we LOVE oatmeal! We'll eat JUST oatmeal if we can stay!" It became a real favorite place for us to go on vacation... to go up to Kelly Lake.

Another time we were going up there, we carried our stuff. Every one had their own pack, even Tom had a little lard pail filled with part of our food for him to carry. We went by foot and, of course since we were walking, we couldn't take quite as much food. We wanted to stay longer after we got up there so Sis and I said if we

The whole family all packed up to go to Kelly Lake about 1924.

can go to town we can charge food at Sloss's store and we'll bring it back. We went to town and went to Sloss's store. We saw right away that they had watermelon. We thought, well, we'll have a real treat for the family. So we bought a watermelon. As I remember, it was three cents a pound. We started back up to Kelly Lake. It was a little hard carrying that big heavy watermelon but we got what was probably about half way, where there was a good spring. We decided we'd put that watermelon in the spring and get it nice and cold, take all the rest of the supplies up to the cabin and come back and get the watermelon. We did that and we had help when we came back. We all walked down to the spring and took the water-melon back up to the cabin.

Martha: A few minutes ago we mentioned Daisy when we were going to Kelly Lake and I've got to tell you a little about how we acquired Daisy. One of our neighbors had this horse and she told daddy that she would sell the horse for ten dollars and... by the way, the horse LOVED apple pie.

Mary: The horse was 22 years old.

Martha: Yes. It was an old horse. Anyway... she said if any children ever fall off of this horse and it doesn't stop you can have your ten dollars back, well... he never got his ten dollars back. We had as many as seven kids on that horse. We'd have them up on the neck clear to the tail and, once in awhile, one would slide off but the horse would always stop. It was a great horse!

Mary: We also had a cow named Rosie. Rosie was greedy and Daisy had poor teeth and had a hard time getting enough food. Rosie had real sharp horns. She was a MEAN old cow. So one day after the grass was cut, Sis was going to get in the pasture and give the grass to the horse. We didn't want Rosie to have it. So Sis went clear across the pasture with this basket of grass for Daisy. Rosie saw her and came running.   Mom was at the fence and said, " Drop the grass! Drop the grass! " Sis said, "No, I don't want Rosie to get this grass." So she came running back to the fence with the basket and got there just in time to get over the fence.

   A man had a dog that he wanted to find a good home for so he brought it to us and he said that the dog's name is Bolshevik. He said," He doesn't suck eggs." (a dog that "sucks eggs" is one that sneaks into the hen house and eats the eggs) So Daddy took the dog and, lo and behold, the dog did suck eggs. So Daddy thought he knew a good way to get rid of that habit so he filled an empty egg shell with hot pepper and gave it to Bolshevik. That stopped the egg sucking habit!

Martha: Speaking of animals, it reminds me of the time there was a bummer lamb up on the Frying Pan road. Daddy had gone fishing and came home and said there was a little lamb that hadn't been able to keep up with the herd. The herders generally just left the weak ones by the side of the road. So, the next morning early, Mom got up and she took a can of condensed milk....remember, she was a city girl, she didn't know anything about animals...and she took off. Well, when Daddy woke up and found that she was gone, he just surmised that something like that had happened so he went up the

Frying Pan and he found her. She had found the lamb and she had the milk but she had no idea how she was going to give it to the lamb. Daddy carried the lamb home and showed us how to teach the lamb to drink from a bottle. Luckily we had a bottle with a nipple in the house. A lamb does not automatically know how to get milk from a bottle. First Daddy dipped his finger in milk and put his finger in the lamb's mouth. When the lamb tasted the milk and started to suck on his finger, then he substituted the nipple for his finger. Soon the lamb got the idea and drained the bottle in no time.

We raised that bummer lamb and she became quite a pet. We called her Patsy. A neighbor of ours had a dog, Bruce. They would say, "Round the house, Bruce" and Bruce would run around the house and jump over a stick they would hold up between the house and the fence. We taught our lamb, Patsy, to do the same trick. The lamb was such a pet, in the fall when it came time to butcher the lamb, Daddy knew that there was no way that we could stand to eat Patsy so he traded the lamb to one of our neighbors for a dozen roasting chickens.

Mary: We've told you quite a lot about Daddy. He was quite a self-sufficient person. He did a lot of things. One thing, he had a last for mending shoes and he would put soles on all of our shoes, the whole family. Also he had a whet stone or grinding wheel that is used to sharpen axes and garden tools and knives and this sort of thing. We always helped with various chores around the yard and house and when he sharpened tools, Sis was the one to turn the grinder.

Martha: Yes, I remember that!

Mary: Daddy held the blade on the grinding wheel and I got the easy job of just pouring on the water. Sis always thought I should help a little bit more than that.

Another one of the things that he did that was self -sufficient was, he knew how to take care of bees. One time a swarm came into our apple tree. We had a hive and he got the bees into the hive. Daddy wore his coveralls, his gloves and a hat with a veil. He held a box under the swarm and carefully brushed the bees off the branch into the box. He had to brush them gently so they wouldn't get mad. Daddy told us that when bees are in a swarm they are very full of honey they are taking with them and they usually don't sting but he was prepared anyway. He put the bees into the hive and soon we had honey right at home.

Other times, he and some other fellows would go out in the wild and find a "bee tree" and take some of the wild honey.

Another thing that Daddy knew how to do was to smoke hams and bacon. He had a little house built that he could close up when the meat or whatever was smoking was in it. In those days they used a lot of curing salt ...I suppose it was a salt. We didn't care much for the ham and bacon because it tasted too salty but it was important meat for those days when you didn't have refrigeration.

Another one of the jobs he taught Mom how to do was to make soap. When they butchered a hog they would make the soap. They cut all the fat off the hog carcass and put it in a big kettle over a fire. This was all done outside. They added lye and boiling water to the kettle of melted fat. Daddy said," You kids stand back now! This hot fat is gonna spit!" When they were making the soap they made a real strong soap like the old Felsnaptha that was used for boiling up the washing. Then they made soap with rose water and glycerine that was pleasant for hand soap and had no lye in it.

Martha: And that was also for our baths, and by the way, we took our baths in the kitchen. There would be a big tub of water. We didn't each have a fresh tub of water but...

Mary: Sometimes one of us or the other would 'dibbsy' for first.

Martha: Yes, and so all of us would have our bath on Saturday night. Everybody had a bath in front of the kitchen stove where it was warm.

Mary: And one time Sis was right close to the stove and...our stove was one of those stoves that had nickel trim...and there was a design on the door where you put in the wood and that door fell

The Saturday Night Tub

Dr. Martin T. Bergsjo

Today things are so modernized
And everything is so tame,
It is hard to recall a few years back
Running Water was an Indian's name.

In those days the only showers
Watered tree and shrub.
Our baths were taken regularly
Each Saturday night, in a tub.

Now this tub had no bright spout
From which the water came gushing.
It was just the round old galvanized thing
That was used for Monday's washing.

Two buckets of water from out of the pump
And one steaming kettle was our quota,
Whether it turned out too hot or too cold
It mattered not a single iota.

And no privacy of a bathroom was ours,
To wash ourselves as we were wishin',
Each bath was under the critical eyes
Of our folks, right out in the kitchen.

open on her bottom when she was drying close to the stove and she had quite a scar there.....

Martha: I was BRANDED!

Mary:....for a long time.

Martha: Speaking of taking our baths, we had our baths on Saturday night, then on Sunday morning we would get ready for church...

Mary: ...and we always wore white bloomers for Sunday. (Martha: Oh yes!) Our grandmother from Ohio sent us bloomers she had made out of sateen, black bloomers for during the week and white bloomers for Sunday.

Martha: Well, one Sunday we wanted to go to see some cider making up on the hill. Some people had a cider mill. Mom said we could go but we were to be back in plenty of time for church. Well, we got so interested in the cider that we didn't get back on time. When we got back Mom was really upset. She started out.. ..she got a little switch...and she started with Tommy. He was the youngest and she gave him about one little switch. And then Virginia probably had two little switches. Then she switched Mary a little bit. Finally she started on me, but then, just after she switched me a little bit she decided she needed a brand new switch so she got a brand new one and finished up with me on the brand new switch.

Mary: One morning when we were getting ready for church Tom and Virginia were still asleep so Mom decided that they would probably sleep until we got back from church. She left them sleeping and the rest of us all went to church. The preacher had just started his sermon when up the steps came Virginia and Tom. Virginia had managed to get into her clothes pretty well although they weren't buttoned up. Tom was barefooted and he had on his long underwear with the pants down in the back. They came down the aisle and when Mom and Daddy saw them one took one by the hand and one took the other and they headed for home.

Martha: I can remember Mary and I were so embarrassed we could hardly stand it!

Mary: Money was rather scarce in those days but once in a while we would have a penny to spend. There was a General Store down at the foot of the hill where we could go down to buy penny candy. Once in a while we were able to do that. My favorite candy was the little wax bottles with sweet colored liquid in them and Sis's favorite was black licorice.

Martha: Probably the biggest event of my life, back then, was the time Mom sent me to the store to get a cake of yeast. (fresh yeast

was sold by the 1 inch square cake, not dry yeast in an envelope like they sell it today) In those days yeast cost...she gave me a nickel and I think the yeast was probably three cents or four cents and so in change I got back this penny and when I got home I noticed ...or Mom noticed... that it was a five dollar gold piece. And Mom said, "Well, you'll have to take it back to Mr. Sloss and tell him because someone will be missing that money". So I took it back and he was very surprised that he had given it to me and that somebody had given it to him. He said, " Well, I'll take this and if nobody calls for it...(I don't remember how long he said but a month or so).... then you can have it". Nobody ever called for it and I got the five dollar gold piece.

Jimmy

30

Mary: Sis, do you remember the time Mom had to be gone for a couple of days and Daddy was taking care of us kids? Virginia had very fine hair that got tangled very easily so rather than hurting her by brushing it, he shaved her head clear off and, from then on, she got the nickname of Jimmy because she looked just like a little boy.

Also while she was gone, Daddy fixed some garden turnips and we said we didn't like turnips. He said, "Oh, you'll love these little baby turnips because I'll boil them just right and they'll be buttered!" And we loved those little baby turnips.

Martha: We had kerosene lamps in those days because there was no electricity. Only Mom and Daddy could light the kerosene lamps and we were not to touch them. Once in a great while, not very often, Daddy and Mom would both be gone for an afternoon and into the evening and so there were two things we could do. We were given some cheese which we could carve. We could always carve cheese and we loved to do that...

Mary: and we would eat the cheese after we carved it.

Martha: But when it got dark, we were not to light the lights, so what we would do...we had a big rocking chair and we'd all four get in the rocking chair and rock and sing and wait till they got home.

Mary: Since we didn't have electric lights, when we had our Christmas tree, the only light that we had on it was real candles. They were just lit very briefly....maybe just once during the whole holiday season because it was too dangerous. One year Daddy said he didn't think we'd have a Christmas tree that year. We were pretty upset about that so when the school said they didn't need the tree that they had at school Sis and I decided we would take our sled and go over and get that tree. Well, it was pretty cold weather and it was on toward evening but we went over and got the tree and came back with it. It was so cold that when we got home I had frozen one of my fingers. In those days, for freezing parts like that, Daddy said the best thing to do was rub it in snow. That's what we did for my finger but it turned purple and the skin came off and for a long time I didn't have feeling in that one finger.

Martha: One job that Mary and I both had was with some people by the name of Ellis.

Mary: He had the lettuce shed.

Martha: You see, during World War I all of the farmers in the valley had been making good money raising potatoes but after the war there was less demand for potatoes. A Mr. Ellis moved to Basalt and promoted the idea of raising head lettuce up the valley. The farmers were sold on the lettuce idea so Mr. Ellis built a lettuce packing shed at Wingo Junction. (Wingo Junction is about 3 miles south of Basalt on the road toward Aspen). They grew beautiful lettuce from Basalt clear up to Woody Creek but the project failed because the lettuce never did arrive at its destination in good shape. During that time, Mom had a job working at the lettuce shed.

The Ellis's needed a baby sitter once in a while and so they would hire Mary and me. They told us that we were welcome to listen to their radio. (Mary: the first one in town!) It was the first radio in the town and it was an Atwater Kent. It was so exciting to think you could listen to it but when you turned it on you would hear some people talking and it wasn't very clear, plus it whistled and carried on (Mary: No real programs.) and so it really wasn't that great.

While we're still talking about our days in Basalt, Mom's mother Beatrice, who wasn't very well, came from Ohio to live with us about that time. Her elderly husband, Eli Hull, had fallen down the stairs. He was a man nearly twice our grandmother's age but he had been very agile. He was 99 and was going to be 100 very shortly but he fell down the back stairs. They had lived in a big three story house that was on a big city block. He was a very wealthy man and he left adequate money to our grandmother while she was living but the rest of the money was to go to the city of Newark after she was dead.

Mary: Mom used to say that if she hadn't been such an independent kind of a person she probably would have been fixed for life because when she and my father were divorced she went back East to visit one time. Mr. Hull would have been very willing to have her come there and live but she didn't want to do that.

She didn't want to have anyone in charge of her life so she elected to go it on her own. She probably gave up more or less a fortune in so doing.

Martha: While our grandmother was living with us... she was not poor, she had quite a little money, to us it was a lot of money... she told us kids that we could have one thing. We had to think about it. Our first thought was a bicycle but then we thought, Virginia and Tommy probably wouldn't be old enough to get much good out of a bicycle. Then we thought of a wagon, well that would be fine for Tommy and Virginia but Mary and I didn't think that would be too good for us. Finally we settled on a porch swing...a garden swing...out under the tree. We chose a garden swing and that was for everybody.

Grandmother Beatrice hadn't been in Basalt very long when she became ill and died. L.L. Wilkes was the undertaker. He drove his hearse down to Basalt from Aspen. The hearse had two flat tires on the way to the cemetery because the road was so bad. He had to drive on the rims. We didn't know about it until later.

Mary: The Basalt school had outdoor toilets... also outdoor sheds for the horses. I had a friend, Kathryn Bates, who always insisted when you went to the outhouse that you had to sit on the toilet for five minutes because you dripped that long and she thought we should be clean. I hated to take all that time away from our play-time but I thought since she was a little older than I was, I would go along with it.

Mom took some of us girls on a camping trip up Last Chance. To get to Last Chance we went up the Frying Pan road to the Taylor Creek turnoff, then 4 or 5 miles up Taylor Creek. Daddy and Tom stayed home. While we were up there we built a fire and it was too near the root of a tree. In the night it blazed up, almost burning a pine tree but with all of us carrying water from the creek we got it out.

While we were on that camping trip, Daddy promised Tom that he would take him on a camping trip as soon as we got home. They went on their camping trip and they took Daisy and the two-wheeled cart. They went way up on the Crown. The Crown is a large mesa southeast of Carbondale. They drove Daisy down to Catherine Store and turned left. Then they went south across the bridge and the railroad track. That's where the trail to the Crown took off. Daddy had a mining claim up there that he liked to go to occasionally and see if he could make it a paying thing. They had been gone for about a week. When it was time for them to come home, he had hitched up the horse and packed up the things and they were heading toward home when Daddy just fell out of the wagon. He had had a heart attack or apoplexy. Tom was about six years old but he realized immediately that his father was dead so he tied up Daisy and headed down the road to try to get help. He ran most of the way, but he wasn't able to run all the way because it was about six miles to the nearest farmhouse. He got there and they spoke a foreign language because a lot of the settlers were from Italy but they realized that he needed help and they had a telephone. So Tom went in to use the telephone and he called Marvin Sloss because he said he was afraid that Mom would be too upset if he called her. So he called Marvin and told him what had happened and then help went out to get Mr. McNeil. He had died just suddenly at the age of 74.

At the time of Daddy's death, there was an opening for manager of the telephone office in Basalt...it was a contract office. A contract office provided a salary and living quarters for the manager and her family. The manager was responsible for the office 24 hours a day and she could hire any help she needed. India Lucksinger had the office at that time. She loved to go to the dances and dance all night so she would hire Sis or me, or... there was another girl or two that sometimes would do the job, and we would stay all night. We would lock the office at nine o'clock. There was a cot there where we could sleep but we would answer the phone calls that came in during the night... there was a buzzer. One time when I was working at the office I answered a call in the middle of the night. Of course my voice was kind of small...a young person, I was just in fourth grade... about ten years old. There was a man on the other end of the line.

He said, "Miss, how old are you?" and I told him how old I was. He said, "Young lady, I'm not going to scold you but I will be speaking to the manager." That was when the manager job in the telephone office became available. Our mother took over the office a week after Daddy's funeral. Sis and I both knew how to operate the switchboard so we could help her learn that and the bookwork she had to figure out by herself.

Martha: When Mom went into the telephone office there was one room in the back for a bedroom and another room sort of built on for a kitchen. It was very small and not only did our family live there but my friend, Virginia Crowley, lived with us. Her family lived way up the Frying Pan at Thomasville and she wanted to go to high school in Basalt. Of course she was helpful because she helped run the switchboard. All of us helped with the cooking and helped with the board. One thing I remember, all of our life, up until then, we had had OATMEAL for breakfast 360 days out of 365 and probably Cream of Wheat the other 5 days. What we wanted was some Puffed Rice or Puffed Wheat so...in those days people came to town selling things... Mom bought a great big package of Puffed Wheat for us. We thought that was the greatest thing in the world...I know, it wasn't as good for us as OATMEAL ... but we loved it.

Mary: Another big change in our eating habits was...the Carlson's Drugstore there in Basalt made ice cream sodas. Occasionally we would go down and get ice cream sodas for our whole family for our dessert. That was a rare treat!

Martha: We mentioned a little while ago about Mom getting the contract manager job at the telephone company. Well, she only had that job for about a year when they decided to convert Basalt to dial phones. Before dial phones, it was necessary to "call Central". The central switchboard connected the caller to the party he was calling. Many people were on the same line called "party lines" and they identified their own calls by a specific pattern of rings. Of course some busy bodies listened in on other people's conversations and passed the gossip along to their neighbors. Interestingly

Virginia with Wilkes Hardware and Mortuary in background. Wilkes was the ground floor of the Collins Block building.

Tom in front of the telephone building where we lived upstairs.

enough, Basalt was the very first town in the state to be dialed.

So the telephone company gave Mom the choice to transfer either down valley... Silt or some place, I'm not sure...or Aspen and, of course, we took Aspen. So we moved to Aspen and our family lived upstairs...the telephone office was upstairs above what, at that time, was Healey's Market. We lived in an apartment behind the telephone office. This apartment was much bigger and nicer than what we'd had in Basalt. It had a bedroom for Mom right behind the telephone office. There was a large living room with a daybed - that's where Tommy slept. I guess Virginia had a daybed too. The apartment had a combination dining room/bedroom with a Murphy bed that was large enough for Mary and me. A Murphy bed folds up against the wall in the daytime and looks like a mirrored cabinet. At night it is pulled down and becomes a bed. The kitchen was big and our family usually ate there. The apartment also had a good sized bathroom and plenty of closet space.

Next to Healey's Market was Wilkes Hardware. Across the street from us at that time was Beck and Bishops Store... downstairs ...

Mary: And the Wheeler Opera House was above Beck and Bishops Store. But, remember, in those days, that was in the 1930's, the opera house had been gutted by fire many years before and there were no performances when we lived there.

Martha: One of the advantages of living in Aspen over Basalt was that there was a lady who gave piano lessons. Mom thought that was something that we should definitely have, all of us. So we all started out taking lessons with Mrs. Beck...Ella Beck her name was...and she was great. She played all the music to go with the movies...they were silent movies but she knew how to play something if the horses were coming or if the hero was dying...she had tunes for everything. Well, anyway, we all started out taking lessons. I did not practice. I was not good at it and when I would go to my lesson I would do whatever she wanted me to do and she would say, "Oh, you're just doing great!" and I knew I was not doing great at all. I had not looked at it since the last time and she was not fooling me. So, soon I quit. Well, it wasn't very long before Mary followed my footsteps and quit and Tommy quit but Virginia was good at music. She was always good and she practiced and she did very well. We all loved to hear her play and we didn't even mind it too much when we were supposed to do chores around the house and Virginia wouldn't do any of the work.

Mary: and Mom always said, 'if you had wanted to take lessons...

Martha: No. Virginia would say "I have to practice!" We didn't mind too much but Mom always said, 'Well, if you had wanted to take lessons you could be practicing too." Virginia stuck with the music and we thought she was terrific. We didn't care too much that she didn't do her share of the work.

Mary: So she didn't learn to do anything about cooking except learn to make cocoa and bean salad and later when she got married that was the only thing she knew how to make.

Martha with Ned Parson's skis.

Martha: Yes. She could make good bean salad and cocoa. The Collins Block was the building next to the telephone office. It had apartments upstairs and Wilkes Hardware and Mortuary downstairs. One of the families that lived upstairs was Ora Ware and her three children.

One girl, Dorothy, was the same age as I was and Ethel was Virginia's age and we became very friendly with the whole family and Mrs. Ware ....I don't know if she knew anything about working the switchboard but she knew how to take care of us kids...and Mom had to leave to go to Denver to do some kind of work that had to do with the telephone company so Mrs. Ware took care of us kids and , of course, when Mom was gone, what should happen, well, the mumps came around...and everybody had the mumps except well....go back...we were quarantined whenever we had any childhood disease in those days. You were quarantined until everybody was over them...well, at first it was sort of a lark, I was out of school and I wasn't very sick, but, finally, everybody had had the mumps except Mary and Ethel and we wanted them to get the mumps and get over with it so we could get out of quarantine.

Mary: So, one whole day Ethel and I spent exercising vigorously so that we would wear down our resistance and get the mumps. One thing we did was that Russian dance where you stoop down and push your legs out and cross your arms and we did that until we were exhausted and it worked. The next morning I had the mumps and I was sicker than any of the others. Ethel had them but not quite that bad.

Martha: Mary looked like a chipmunk. She swelled up on one side and then she swelled up on the other side and finally she swelled up on both sides and she was a sight to behold.

Mary: Aspen, in those days, looked very different. The streets weren't paved like they are now. Main street was graveled but all of the side streets were grass except for tracks made by an occasional car. Some streets still had wooden side-walks which had sur-vived from Aspen's glory days during the silver boom before 1893. Many houses were vacant and in poor repair. There were irrigation ditches running beside almost every street in town and

Tom and Virginia

39

Mary

the afternoon showers caused quite a rush of water down each side of the street.

Martha: It was interesting, there were so few people in Aspen in the late 1920's and early 30's that everybody knew everybody. We lived upstairs and if we looked out the window and saw a car we didn't happen to recognize we'd say, "Well I wonder who's in town? Who has relatives visiting?"

The Girls

Mary: This was back before the days of the tourist on-rush and skiing in Aspen as it is today, but we did learn to ski. The telephone company had two pairs of skis that Ned Parsons used for repairing the lines clear up on Independence Pass. They were about nine feet long and four inches wide and they had just straps across the insteps. We learned to ski on those huge skis. We would walk up to the top of Mill Street, the street where the opera house is. We would put the skis on and glide as far down the street as we could. I don't think

Virginia

any of us ever made it as far as the Hotel Jerome. When we fell, the skis flew on down. We had to walk down to pick them up.

Martha: And I remember one time when we were skiing and it was just when people started having bindings on their skis. A friend of ours, Doris Sheehan, was skiing with us down Mill Street. We were using the kind of skis that just had straps across the insteps that Mary was just talking about. Somebody had heard about these bindings that you could use to fasten your skis on so they wouldn't come off. Doris said, "You wouldn't catch me

Aspen 1932. Mary in the white sweater. Virginia 2nd from the left in the back row.

fastening my feet into something like that, if you fell down you'd kill yourself!" Well, of course later she became a very good skier but not without using bindings.

Mary: When we first skied in Aspen there were no tows. We would walk up from the Midnight Mine on the back of Aspen Mountain and ski down the front and it was an all day job. You were pretty well finished up when you'd had just one run of skiing in those days.

Martha: During the war, on the weekends, the soldiers from Camp Hale used to come to Aspen to go skiing. Camp Hale was the headquarters of the 10th Mountain Division during World War II. The base was located on the eastern side of Vail Pass not far from Frisco. In those days, to get to the top of the ski run, we used what was called a 'boat tow'. It looked a little like a boat and you put your skis and poles in the bottom and you sat on the sides. It went up along a cliff and sometimes it would get a little close to the edge and they'd say, "Everybody lean!" and we leaned into the hill because if that thing went over it would hang on the cable and it was very hard to get it back on track. In an afternoon we would probably make twenty or twenty-five runs because it was a very short ski hill. We'd get to the top and the guys would throw the skis helter skelter out of the boat. We would round up our own skis and get them on and in those days you didn't just step into bindings like you do today, it took some effort to put them on. Then we'd ski down, take them off again, put them back in the boat tow and go up for another run. By the end of the day we could wring the water out of our gloves. We were soaked but we had a lot of fun.

The Good Old Days

Additional Recollections
from 1918-1927
in Basalt, Colorado

SCARCE RELATIONS

Mary: Thinking about the way things were in those days... relatives were scarce. Our mother and father were both only children and we didn't know much about our relatives except we thought they were

Grandmother Nora in Leadville, Colorado about 1910.

really OLD. When our mother had to leave our father because of gambling and because of him becoming violent, Grandmother Nora must have been a caring person because she took us in. She had hoped Ed, her son, would settle down and be a good provider. When he was growing up, he had always been a problem to her. Probably that is why she sent him to military school.

Grandmother Downer, Leadville, Colorado.

Soon after Mom married Tom McNeil and we moved to Basalt, Mom got news from Nora that she had committed her son, Ed, (our father) to the State Mental Hospital in Pueblo.

Apparently his schizophrenic behavior had become so serious that she felt Ed could no longer function in society. Our father remained in the State Mental Hospital until his death forty years later. Mom said she would probably never have remarried had she realized that his behavior was caused by mental illness. When we were growing up, our mother went to Pueblo and talked to Ed's doctors. They assured her his illness was not hereditary so if we married and had children it would not be a problem. While visiting with the doctors at the State Mental Hospital, Mom found out how our father was getting along. She found out that he was not locked up all the time. He was a trustee and was allowed quite a bit of freedom. Mom sensed from what the doctors told her that he was not unhappy.

Grandmother Nora was in her early 60's when she died. After Nora's death, her sister in law, Charlotte Downer, our great aunt, came to Aspen to check on the possibility of Sis becoming conservatrix (guardian) of our father's estate which Nora, his mother, had left to him. Aunt Charlotte explained that if the estate had to be put into the hands of a lawyer the money would probably be gone before we were all through college. When she talked to Mom, Aunt Charlotte was pleased to learn that Sis was a good student and seemed capable to take on the responsibility of conservatrix. Charlotte herself was on the board of directors of the bank in Boulder, Colorado and her husband, Frank, was in charge of the US Mint in Denver.

When Aunt Charlotte was visiting us, she told us quite a bit about her daughter, little Charlotte, who was a student at Colorado University. I realized from what Aunt Charlotte said that little Charlotte had had an easy life, never wanting for any-thing. I couldn't help feeling a little envious. I wonder if Aunt Charlotte sensed this because when she went home she packed up some beautiful clothes and some jewelry of little Charlotte's and sent them to us.

Another one of our great aunts was Emily. When her husband, Alfred Dodge Cole, a professor of science in Cincinnati, died, Aunt Emily decided to move to Florida to a retirement residence. Before she moved farther away, she came out west to visit us. Virginia was married by that time and she invited all the family to her house in Aspen for dinner. I don't remember much about great aunt Emily except that she simply poured salt on every-thing on her plate. She dumped the salt on before she even tasted any of it.

Another great aunt was Florence Brewer of Hartford, Connecticut. We never saw her and, to tell you the truth, I don't even remember just how she was related to us but she always sent Mom seventy five dollars every Christmas. One day a regis-tered letter arrived for us. The surprise in it was Florence Brewer's sixteen page will with Mom inheriting fifteen thousand dollars worth of New York Life stock and all of the rest of us another fifteen thousand dollars worth of New York Life to be divided among us except Tom. She either had never heard about him or didn't want it to go to anyone except blood relatives because he wasn't included. Thirty thousand dollars was a great deal of money in those days, maybe not to Florence Brewer because our inheritance was just a very small part of her sixteen page will, but to Mom it looked like her worries for providing all of us with a college education were over. As it turned out, we got to feel like "rich folk" for only a few months, then came the stock market crash and most of the inheritance was gone overnight.

THE FIRE

Mary: In 1918, our first home in Basalt was the Fahey house. Mom was fixing pancakes one morning for breakfast when she realized she was out of butter. She said," Mary, you're a fast runner, will you run down to Mrs. White's and borrow some butter?" As I started into our yard on my way back I saw the most beautiful red-orange wavy color on the ceiling in our kitchen. I put down the butter dish so I could run and see what was happening. It was the ceiling wallpaper on fire. Mom and Daddy were trying to put it out. Mom had a bucket of water and Daddy had the hose fastened to the pump outside our back door. The Fahey house had no inside plumbing and the town had no fire fighting equipment. Neighbors seeing fire always came on the run with buckets. Sometimes they formed a line from the river and used a bucket brigade. Our fire was quickly put out and the stove was still warm so we sat down to have breakfast. But, where was the butter? We looked and looked. Where we finally found it was behind the tree. I had set it down before I ran to see what was going on. That was a very fortunate experience with fire.

THE OUTHOUSE

Martha: I think we mentioned earlier that when we lived in the Fahey house we didn't have indoor plumbing. We had an outhouse. One of the problems we had was, in the winter, when we were wearing all of our heavy clothes and mittens and all that, invariably, when we would go to the bathroom, we would drop one of our mittens down the toilet hole. It was particularly bad because we had mittens that were given to us. They were hand knit and they were beautiful mittens. Either Mary or I, I don't know about the little kids, but invariably either Mary or I would drop one of our mittens down the toilet. Then we'd have to call Daddy and have him come and help us get the mitten out of the toilet. Even though it happened numerous times, he never seemed to lose patience with us. He would get a long stiff wire, bent up on the end into a hook, and a kerosene lantern and he would go out and fish the mitten out of the hole. Each time it happened, he would caution us to be more careful with our mittens the next time.

WE WERE SELF-SUFFICIENT

Martha: Mary mentioned earlier that daddy smoked hams and bacon. In 1923, when we moved into the house we bought from John White, we had a good sized cellar. There was a trapdoor in the kitchen to get to it. Soon after moving into that house we bought the block across the street from us. This provided us with a place to have a large garden. We raised radishes, onions and lettuce. These came on early. We also had root vegetables; carrots, turnips, potatoes. We also raised corn, beans, peas, tomatoes, squash and cucumbers. The green beans were pole beans that were staked with tall willow poles, tepee style. Mary and I had to help with that, also we had to stake the pea vines. Mom canned green beans, corn and peas. They were tricky to can because they were nonacid. She had no pressure cooker. They were canned by what is called the water bath method. The jars were filled and placed in a boiler and covered with water about an inch over the tops and boiled for about an hour. She also canned the tomatoes. The root vegetables were stored in sand in the cellar.

We built a chicken coop on the block across from us. We had plenty of eggs and freshly killed chicken but Mom canned chicken also. We had rabbit hutches in our back yard and fried rabbit was a common meal for us. About once a year daddy would buy a hog and butcher it. Then Mom cooked the pork chops and put them in a big crock, probably 10 gallon size. The pork chops were covered with lard to keep the air away from them. When we wanted some for a meal we scraped the lard back and took out the chops, being very careful to seal the lard around the remainder.

One thing we really liked was dried corn. The corn was cooked, cut off the cob and dried in the oven till it was just browned. We liked it just that way, or cooked in milk. We had some apple trees and Mom made apple sauce and canned it. We were pretty self-sufficient.

VIRGINIA'S SIXTH BIRTHDAY

Our 2nd home in Basalt. John White house. (Purchased for $500.00 about 1923.) Mary and Tom sitting on the front steps of the White house.

Martha: Well, in 1923, we had some friends, the Whites, who had decided to move to Denver and wanted to sell their house in Basalt. They sold it to us for $500 and maybe they let us buy it on time. I don't know, but anyway, in 1923 we moved into that house. I remember, it was Virginia's sixth birthday. She had a friend, her name was Edie Mae Powell, and Edie Mae took it upon herself on that day to invite all of Virginia's friends to a birthday party. I remember, one of the kids that came, a little boy named Charles Dixon Harris. Virginia liked him real well. I don't remember who the other children were but, anyway, here we were in the midst of moving and you can imagine the confusion. Well, we sat on the steps, on the porch of the new house and had Virginia's sixth birthday party.

Now we were in a new house that had indoor plumbing but it only had one bedroom. Daddy and Mom and the two little kids slept in the bedroom and Mary and I slept in a bed on the back porch. Mary said that was great because we could talk about things we didn't

Daddy and Uncle Harry and all the kids in the front yard of the White house.

Second home in Basalt (John White House)
Virginia, Tommy, Mary, Martha with wealthy apple
tree in the backyard.

want the little kids to hear. We loved sleeping out on the screen porch in the summer because it was so cool with fresh air blowing through but in the winter it was cold. We heated up Mom's clothes irons called "sad irons" (what made them feel so unhappy?) and wrapped them in towels to keep our feet warm. We used to sleep with our heads under the covers so our noses wouldn't get cold.

OUR FRIENDS, THE BATES FAMILY

Martha: When we were growing up in Basalt our best friends were the Bates family. They had four girls. Norma and I were about the same age, as were Mary and Kathryn, and Virginia and Barbara. Then they had a little sister. She was a little younger than Tommy. We were very close. We had a lot of fun. The way we met them in the first place was that Norma's grandmother was our neighbor in Basalt. Norma's family lived on the Wheatley ranch on the Roaring Fork River about a mile above Old Snowmass. On Norma's ninth birthday her grandmother thought it would be nice if I should meet Norma so she asked if they would like to have me come to Norma's birthday party. She took me there. I had a wonderful day with them and I met the whole family. Later, not much later, they moved to Basalt and we were friends for many years.

One of the things that happened with Norma and I was the time that we cut our hair. Going back a little ways, it was starting to be the "fad" all over the United States that women were bobbing their hair. Mom thought she would like to have hers cut and she said," I think I would like to have my hair cut." She didn't know if Daddy would approve of it, not everybody did it. But anyway, she made the comment she'd like to cut her hair and Daddy said, "Well, if I were a woman and I wanted to cut my hair, I would cut it!" So Mom bobbed her hair. She was about the first lady in Basalt to do so. A little later, I wanted to have my hair cut. I wore it in braids and I wanted to have it cut. Norma, my friend, had beautiful long hair that came almost to her waist. She generally wore it in braids. Norma said, "Oh, wouldn't it be great if we could cut our hair?" And so we asked our parents. I was sure Mom would let me do it. Norma's mother said, "Well, if Martha's mother cuts her hair then I'll cut your hair." So Mom did cut my hair. Then we went down to Norma's and told her mother. She saw I had my hair cut. She said,"Oh well, since I promised I'd do it, I will!" She got the scissors and cut off one of Norma's braids. Then she burst into tears and ran into the bedroom and, there was Norma with only one braid cut off. We didn't know what to do. I said, "Why don't we go up to my house and let Mom finish cutting your hair?" Norma said, "Oh, I couldn't do that." Well, we just waited a while and finally her mother came out of the bedroom and wiped her tears and finished cutting her hair. It was really quite a thing.

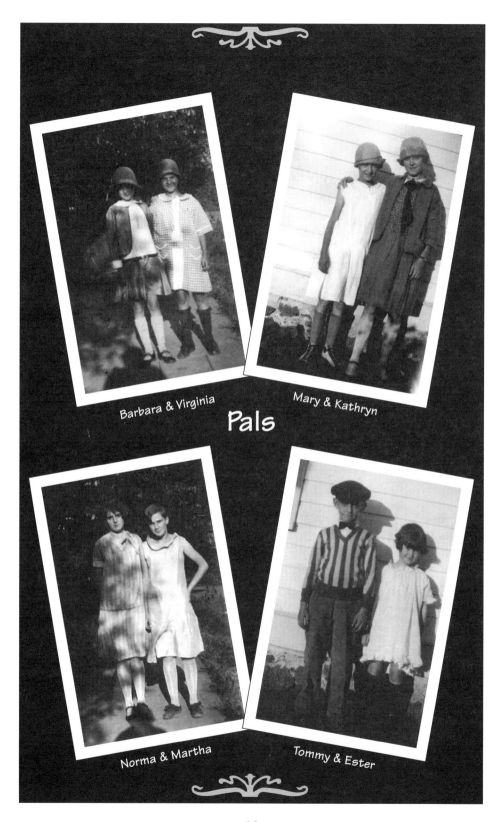

Barbara & Virginia

Mary & Kathryn

Pals

Norma & Martha

Tommy & Ester

Barbara Bates, 1926

Kathryn Bates, 1926

Bates Girls

Norma Bates, 1926

Ester Bates, 1926

PRANKS

Martha: Well, I don't know whether we were any different from any other kids but it seemed like we used to love to play pranks on people. One time Mom was entertaining Literary Club and Tommy wasn't very old but, he was old enough to know better. Anyway, we had a range in the kitchen that was always going, it was always hot. Tommy sprinkled pepper on the range. All the ladies began coughing and sneezing and carrying on. I don't remember whether Mom just opened the doors and everybody recovered or whether they all had to go home. I think they just opened the doors and it was OK.

Another time, it was April Fool's Day, and I think we mentioned before that our Daddy thought that everybody should have oatmeal for breakfast every day of the world. So, of course, we were going to have oatmeal. Mary and I thought, the night before April Fool's Day, let's put salt in the sugar bowl and sugar in the salt shaker and have a big joke. Daddy always dished up the oatmeal at breakfast time but he generally just passed it to us and we put our own sugar and cream on it. For some reason on that April Fool's morn-

Sorosis Literary Club
Front row: Georginia Bates, Mrs. Williams (7th & 8th grade teacher),
Rachel Sloan Hyrup, Mom. Second row: Mother Bates, Ruth Nash,
Alma Harris, Hazel Hyrup (Washington's birthday party)

ing, (and I don't think he knew it but it just happened), after he dished up the oatmeal, he started to put the sugar on it and Mary and I said, "We don't want any sugar!" and he said, "Of course you want sugar!" So he put it on and passed it to us and pretty soon it was evident that something was wrong because we weren't eating it but he had already dished everybody's. Well then Tommy started to eat his oatmeal. He made a face and said he couldn't eat it because it was too salty. By then, Daddy had caught on and he told Tommy he didn't need to eat his oatmeal because he knew very well that Tommy had nothing to do with the prank. And then he said Virginia didn't need to eat hers. She probably didn't have anything to

Tom the Prankster

do with it either. But, he said to Mary and me, " Eat your oatmeal!" Well, of course, there was no way we could eat it. Finally, after quite a while, he gave us some different oatmeal without salt. We thought it was all solved but then, a little later on in the breakfast, what should happen but Mom put sugar on her eggs! That was a big prank that kind of backfired on Mary and me.

WHAT WE DID FOR FUN

Martha: Since we didn't have any TV or any radio or anything like that we had to make our own fun. One of the things we did was play marbles. I loved to play marbles with the boys. Not many girls did. We also played jacks. All of the kids loved to play jacks. Norma and I were really good at it, especially Norma. She could pick up all ten jacks with one bounce, sometimes. It seemed like every-one in school jumped rope. We all knew dozens of ' jump rope ditties'. Another thing we did was walk on stilts. When we first had our stilts, it was when we still were living in the Fahey House, which was early on, we wanted to have some stilts and Daddy said, sure

Tommy and Virginia goin' fishing.

he'd make us some. So he made them and he said they were ready. I said to him, "Well, they don't have any straps on them, they're sup-posed to have straps on them." He said, "Well, when you learn to walk 'em without straps then I'll put straps on 'em because if you don't know how to do it you're going to get hurt when you fall down so this way when you fall you just take your foot off and you're OK."

So, we did learn to walk the stilts without straps and then we got straps. Well, some of our friends were really good at walking on stilts. The Murray boys, I remember, they would walk up to our house...and this was after we moved down into the house we bought from the White's, from John White...Raymond Murray would walk right up to our house and right onto our porch roof. His stilts were that high he could walk right onto our porch roof! We loved to walk stilts in the spring when it was kind of muddy and there wasn't much else you could do but you could always walk on stilts, even in the mud. Later, when the river went down and it was summer and the water wasn't very high, Mary, sort of on a dare, walked across the river on her stilts. She made it OK.

We used to play games like Run Sheep Run and Hide N Seek and we played a game called Ante Over. You had a basketball and you would throw it over a building and the team on the other side, if they caught it, they would run around the building and try to tag the people on our side. That was a great game. Anyway, that's kind of the way we entertained ourselves.

SCHOOL

Martha: When I started to school in Basalt the school building had four rooms, two downstairs and two upstairs. First, second and third were in one room downstairs and fourth, fifth and sixth were in the other. One room upstairs was seventh and eighth and the other room was high school. My first grade teacher was Dorothy Willits. My school work was fine but I was always in trouble for talking too much. When I received my report card at the end of the month I had a D in deportment. When I got home there was no one home so I put the card on the table and went outside. I stayed outside as long as I could but finally Mom called me to dinner. I went inside expecting the worst but Mom didn't mention the report card. We ate dinner as usual. But after dinner she said, "Martha, I think we need to have a little talk." Mom asked me what I had done

Martha in 1926 wearing the two dresses her mother made for her trip to Denver.

to deserve a D. I said, "Well I don't know of anything I've done but she does get after me a whole lot for talking so maybe that's it." We didn't have a telephone in those days so mom said, "I will have to go talk to your teacher. I'll talk to Dorothy Willits about it." Well so I suffered through it and I didn't know when she'd get to go see Mrs. Willits but she didn't go that night, she went the next day. I had to suffer all that time and the next day when I got home from school, after mom had had a chance to talk to Dorothy Willits, she said, "Well, Mrs. Willits said that you definitely do talk too much. It disturbs the class and it is disrupting." But it wasn't so bad that Mom thought I should have to have a spanking.

Then when I was in the fourth grade my teacher's name was Miss Sadoris. She taught fourth, fifth and sixth. Miss Sadoris was an old maid. The rubber hose was something she really used a lot. She whipped the kids every whip-stitch. One day someone in the fourth grade, in the back of the room, said something under their breath that she didn't like. She said." Whoever said that has got to come forward and admit it." Nobody did. So she said, " Alright, if nobody admits it, I will have to whip everyone in the whole class." Nobody admitted it. She started out with the first one in the row. She called that student up and gave him a little whipping... rubber-hosing... on the bottom. The next one just got up and marched up there and she whipped him. In turn every body went up. It was kind of funny. It didn't hurt very much and we were all kind of laughing under our breath at the whole situation. That was one of the things that happened in fourth grade.

Another thing that happened, I think this was in the fifth grade, one time one of the kids got sick and vomited on the floor right in front of the teacher's desk. And, of course, when anybody got sick the kids were all sort of excited, you know, wondering what to do and what should be done. Miss Sadoris said." Just sit down, be calm and I will take care of it." She said," I can not do it on an empty stomach. I can't clean this up without something to eat." So she went to her lunch box and she got a piece of pie. She brought the pie to her desk and she put a handkerchief sort of around her nose ...on her face, around her nose...and she sat and ate the pie. We were all sitting there at our desks watching this whole thing.

When she finished the pie, I guess that fortified her enough, so she cleaned up the mess.

When we were in the fifth grade, we were always looking forward to being in the sixth grade because the sixth graders got to sit in double desks. They had a row of double desks so two kids could sit together and that looked like great fun to us.

Then, when I was in the seventh grade, I had a teacher by the name of Mrs. Williams. Her son, Lloyd Williams, who was also in her class, sort of had a crush on me.

I remember one time they took me to Glenwood with them and while Mrs. Williams was doing some business, Lloyd and I hiked up the mountain above the Glenwood Hot Springs Pool. When we came back down we went for a swim. At that time, there were large logs floating in the pool. They were there for the swimmers to play on. The logs were covered with slimy green moss and they were VERY slick. Lloyd and I had a contest to see which of us could ride the log the longest without slipping off. One person straddled the log and tried to stay upright while the other person turned the log and tried to tip the rider into the water. Lloyd won! Lloyd bought me a hamburger when we got out of the pool. Then we met up with Mrs. Williams and we all drove home. I suppose Lloyd might be considered to be my first boyfriend.

When I was in the eighth grade, we always had spelling bees. They had one that was county wide. First you had to win in your school. At the same time, we also had an oratorical contest. Well, I entered both of those. I have to admit...I did not write that speech...I might have helped a little but not much... with the writing of my oration. (Mom was very good at that sort of thing.) But I learned it and gave it and I won in our school. I was also one of the ones who got to go to the county spelling bee . We went to the county seat which was over in Eagle. You know, it was pretty exciting for a kid, I'd never been any place before by myself. I didn't do too well in the spelling. I think I was third or fourth or something but I won the oratorical contest. That meant I got to go to Denver. So, since I was going to Denver... you know, you couldn't buy clothes in Basalt, they didn't have a place to buy clothes... Mom made me two dresses and I thought I was really something. Anyway, I went to

Denver. I didn't win in Denver but I didn't feel too bad because the trip itself was so much fun. We stayed at the Shirley Savoy Hotel. It was an exciting experience for me. We went to the zoo. We went to the Mint. We did a lot of things. Probably more exciting than going to the zoo or going to the Mint was the actual trip to Denver because we went on the train. That trip was a highlight of my eighth grade year.

During the summer of 1926, after I was in the eighth grade, was the time that Daddy died. Mom got the job with the telephone company and my friend, Virginia Crowley, whose family lived way up the Frying Pan, stayed with us at the telephone office so she could attend High School. I had one year in the Basalt High School which I don't remember as being anything very exciting but we did go to a few dances and parties. That's what I was more interested in at that time. I remember I went with Troy Williams, no relation to Lloyd Williams. His family had a big ranch up the Frying Pan. What was their ranch is now covered by Ruedi Reservoir. Troy was a few years older than me. He had a car. It was a Star. Troy knew how to dance and he taught me to do the Charleston.

A SELFISH ACT

Martha: One thing that happened that makes me feel bad every time I think about it is a selfish thing I did. Mom wanted to have all of our pictures taken. Since there was no photographer in Basalt, we had to go to Glenwood Springs to have our pictures taken. We dressed in our Sunday best and went to Glenwood for a sitting. Mom picked out the best pictures from the proofs. Rather than individual pictures, she had a panel made with all four of us. When the photo panel came she showed it to us and I didn't like my picture. So, when no one was around, I cut my picture off of the

panel and that, of course, ruined the whole thing. Mom never did go ahead and have it done over or ever display any of those photos even though I thought the other three were very good. I'm sure it was a very big disappointment to her. We didn't have very much money and it probably had cost quite a bit to have it done and she didn't have the picture she wanted. After Mom died and Mary and I were dividing up the family pictures, we came upon the two parts of that panel and Mary said I should take it and I have it to this day. Cutting that photo is one thing that I have regretted for all my life.

NEIGHBORS

Martha: When we lived in the White house, our neighbors next door were the Stones and they were not our favorite neighbors. We kids argued and fought across the fence all the time and Mom said she would be happy when they would be "benefited elsewhere". She meant she would be glad to get rid of them. It wasn't very long after that that they did move and we bought that house.

About this time, Daddy's daughter by his former marriage lost her husband. They had lived in Denver. Her name was Rachel Sloan . She had three children. Madeline, the oldest, was already in college. Bob, who had a muscular disease and was in a wheelchair, was a few years older than me, and Norma, the youngest one, was about Virginia's age. After her husband died, Rachel wanted to move to Basalt so we rented the house we had bought from the Stones to her. Rachel had a car and our families went on a lot of picnics together. We would go on a picnic

Picnic at Rifle Falls, July 4, 1925

about once a week and even if it was stormy, why, we'd still plan the picnic. Mom and Rachel would say," Oh, it'll be fine by afternoon." and it generally was.

Mom and Rachel were great friends. The fact that Daddy's daughter was four years older than his wife never seemed to matter to either of them. Only once that I can remember was the age difference an issue. On Rachel's fortieth birthday Mom made her a cake and on it she wrote, "Fair, Fat and Forty!" Rachel became sort of upset over that cake.

One picnic I remember, we went down to Rifle Falls because Rachel wanted to see where she had grown up. It was a long drive. We spent the whole day and Daddy showed Rachel where she had lived when she was small. We had our picnic at the base of the falls. The falls were so beautiful.

Rachel's car

Our favorite place to picnic was the Park, which is where the Schweppes now live. To get to the Park, go up the Frying Pan road and turn left at Taylor Creek. It's the same road that goes to Last Chance only you get to the Park before you come to Last Chance. The Park was owned, at that time, by Chris and Hazel Hyrup. They had two children, Gene and Annabelle. Gene was exactly a year younger than Mary and Annabelle was about Virginia's age. Later, Chris and Hazel had two more children, Bob and Pat. Anyway, we would go up to the Park and, when we would eat with the Hyrups, Chris would always have venison. He'd get it out of season. We'd have it outdoors and cook it over the fire. It was so good. Later, years later, Rachel married Chris Hyrup's younger brother Alfred and they moved to California.

Speaking of neighbors, one house down, west yet of Rachel's house, was where the Nash family lived . They had lived out on Willits

Lane before their father died and Mrs. Nash, her name was Ruth, belonged to the same club Mom did. For years she used to drive to town in her buggy. She would leave her horse and buggy at our house and they would go to Literary Club and then she would drive home. Her husband, Fred Nash, died and left her with three children. Adriane was my age. Freeman was just a year younger than me and there was a younger brother, Amos, called Happy. They moved into the house just west of where Rachel lived and were really great neighbors. Adriane and I always had a lot of fun together. We would visit back and forth quite a bit.

STRAWBERRY DAYS

Martha: One of the things that we did with the Bates girls is go to Strawberry Days. The Bates girls had an uncle. He was red headed. His name was Bill but they called him Uncle Blue. Well, Uncle Blue was talked into taking us four older girls, Mary, Kathryn, Norma and me, to Strawberry Days. On the way we kept having flat tires. Well, for the first one he had a spare but after that he had to start patching them. So every time one of them would go flat (I think we had about six flat tires on the way), he would have to pull over and patch it. Cars would be going by us on their way to Strawberry Days, making a cloud of dust and, of course, nobody helped or anything. Well, we offered to help but he said... by the way, we were all dressed fit to kill, white dresses, you know, patent leather shoes, all this stuff. Our folks had dressed us up pretty good for Strawberry Day... anyway, he said, "No, you just sit in the car and don't bother me." I was surprised that Uncle Blue didn't lose his temper because he was red headed and he was known for a temper, but he managed to control it and he fixed the tires, one by one. We finally got to Glenwood Springs. During Strawberry Days, at that time, they served fresh strawberries all day long. The strawberries were raised over by Cardiff next to the hill. Apparently that area was warm from special wind currents and they used to raise a lot of strawberries there. The women brought cake so we had real strawberries and cream, real cream, all day long they served that, and cake. Then another thing you could do, you could go in the Glenwood Hot Springs pool for free. You could go in for FREE. So, of course, we took advantage of going in the pool and we stayed until our hands were all puckered up. After the pool we went to the carnival which lined both sides of Grand Avenue. We only tried a couple of games. We did try to throw a ball and win a Kewpi doll but none of us succeeded. Imagine, after spending the whole day at Strawberry Days, we went home with about half of the dollar we each took to spend.

SKATING TO FLORIDA

Mary: Sis, do you remember our big plan to skate to Florida? I think it was when a very strong flood hit Pueblo in the early twenties. Mom had to go to Pueblo, Colorado to see if she could save the building and the skates that our father, Ed Downer, owned there. Daddy said he could manage with us kids, so Mom went.

Right away we thought of planning a trip on roller skates to Florida. We knew we could skate and with Daddy helping Tommy, and Mom helping Virginia we would have a great time.

An engineer friend of Daddy's gave us a map and we planned our route. We decided we would ask him to let us ride on the train where the hills were too tiring, which wouldn't be much of the way. We would not be any bother.

We fixed up a pack for each of us and were about ready when Mom got home with the sad news that everything was sold. We could start saving our money to buy skates.

We did save a lot and Mom thought Santa would help us out, so Christmas day we started to learn to skate on our hard wood floor. In that house you could make a round trip starting in the kitchen, through the living room, the bedroom then the bathroom and right back through the kitchen. The Bates girls had new Christmas skates, too. What a racket! There were eight of us racing around grabbing at the door casings as we whirled by. Norma was on the heavy side. As she went clickety clack through the kitchen, she fell, straddling the kitchen and living room door casing. Daddy tried to help her up but we were all laughing too hard. We thought we would just have to let her stay there.

SATURDAY NIGHT DANCES

Mary: Saturday night dances provided the fun for the area. From Aspen, Woody Creek, Norrie, Basalt, Biglow, Carbondale, down to DeBeque that was the thing for the family's social life. When Sis was about twelve, our whole family went to one in Basalt. At breakfast the next morning, Daddy said if we're going to go to the dances, you girls better learn to dance. We had lots of volunteers helping us practice step, one, two, three, glide...step, one, two, three, glide. Most of the dances in Basalt were in the Odd Fellows Hall, a two story brick building. Lupton's Grocery Store was on the ground floor and upstairs was the dance hall. The chairs were all pulled to the side for the specta-

Troy Williams taught sis to dance.

tors and the cloak room provided space for the little ones to fall asleep on coats or little blankets. Various ladies groups made money by serving supper at about thirty five cents apiece.

The dance bands were from hometowns or bands from other area towns. Virginia, our sister, helped organize one of the Aspen bands. Sis McHugh's was one of the most popular bands. Wilmina and Edwina Sheehan were the mainstays of one dance band.

73

Armand DeBeck had a popular band also. When I was in the seventh grade, they had a waltz contest for the young teenagers. I was hoping Laurent Arbaney would ask me to be his partner as I thought he was the best dancer, but Buster Arbaney was the one to ask me first. The judges eliminated couples by tapping the boys on the shoulder. It was down to three couples when my partner and I were eliminated so we got third place. The top three couples got free suppers.

Once in a while they would have a box supper. The single ladies and young girls would decorate a box and put in supper for two people. The boxes were put on two tables, one for the single ladies and girls and one for the family groups. At supper time they would have an auction. Usually the boxes would go for about fifty cents, but once in a while a box would go for a dollar if the bidding went high for the chance to eat supper with a particularly popular girl. The winner of the box would have supper with the girl who brought the box.

I remember one box supper when I decorated my box with pink and blue paper and ribbons. The boy I had a crush on at that time asked, "What does your box look like?" I told him my box was pink and blue. When they set the boxes out on the table, I was shocked to see two pink and blue boxes. How would he know which one was mine? When the first pink and blue box went up for auction, the cute boy bid on it. I tried to signal him that it wasn't my box, but he kept on bidding. Luckily, the other bidder had more money and got that box. The boy looked over at me as if to say, "Well, I tried." I smiled and pointed to the other pink and blue box. When it came up for bids, he bought it and we ate together.

About 2:00 A.M. the band would play Auld Lang Syne but with plenty of clapping and stamping the band would play a couple of extra numbers.

Life's Loves & Lessons

LeRoy and Martha taken at Norrie in 1929

Recollections
from Aspen, Colorado

WE BECAME BIRD WATCHERS EARLY

Mary: Our family all became bird watchers. It started one day when I was walking to my friend's house. I saw a little humming bird wrapped in fuzz that had fallen out of a nest. The nest was so high I couldn't get the bird back into it so I put the baby hummingbird in my handkerchief and took it home to see if I could take care of it. I had just recently read an article in the National Geographic about how to feed hummingbirds. I found an empty perfume bottle to put sugar and water in for feeding. I made a little nest and put the baby in it and I placed the nest in an open window of our apartment. I left the screen on the window so the bird couldn't fall out. At first I had to hold the bottle to the hummingbirds' bill so it could see what to do. After it learned where the sugar water came from, it could drink from the bottle on its own. When it got stronger I left the screen open and fixed a little perch, sort of a swing, so it could have a place to sit by the window. The baby bird stayed there until it started to fly. Then it flew in and out most every day. It stayed nearly all summer. The following two years it came back occasionally. One day Ora Ware was making a cake and a hummingbird came in the window and sampled the icing. We were sure it was the one I raised. When fall came it migrated again. That's the last we saw of it.

WHAT OUR INHERITANCE BOUGHT

Martha: When we moved to Aspen, we had an icebox for the first time. Ice was delivered once a week. If I remember correctly, Ray Hendricks's father delivered ice. He had a team and wagon. Sometimes we'd get an extra block of ice and make homemade ice cream with an old crank style freezer. About 1929 we finally got an actual refrigerator. This is how that happened.

When we received the inheritance from Florence Brewer that Mary mentioned in Scarce Relations, Mom was bombarded with salesmen wanting her to buy things. I suppose, in that small town, everyone knew we had come into some money. The salesmen, I remember, were trying to sell her a car. They took her driving and let her drive. One salesman was J.V. Rose. He had a Chevrolet dealership in Glenwood where the Tamarack Building is now. Berthod Motors was there for many years after Rose retired. Anyway, Mom thought about it a lot but decided against a car. What she wanted was a refrigerator! The Crosley Shelvador had just come on the market at that time and that is what she bought. That refrigerator was her pride and joy.

The inheritance, as I remember, was in New York Life stock that paid dividends. Mom probably used some of the dividends to buy the Crosley. We banked at the Bank of Aspen. Mr. Berglund was head of the bank. In 1929, just after the stock market crash, Mr. Berglund came to see Mom one evening after work. He told her there were rumors that the bank would have to close. He had figured a way that she might be able to salvage some of the money. Whatever his scheme was they took care of it that night before the bank closed. That's the only reason we had the $40 a month for our education.

THE CONSERVATRIX

Martha: The summer after Aunt Charlotte visited our family in Aspen and she decided, from talking to Mom, that I might have a good enough head on my shoulders to be the guardian of my father's estate, Charlotte arranged for me to meet her in Pueblo. I was going to learn what the actual duties of conservatrix would be. I had never met Aunt Charlotte because, when she came to visit, I was away at college. I started college at age 17 so I was probably 18 when I traveled to Pueblo for the meeting.

When I went to the meeting with Aunt Charlotte, I had to travel, by myself, from Glenwood Springs to Pueblo on the train. I loved the train trip. I was so impressed by the fancy dining car with white linen tablecloths and napkins and the ornate silver service. I ordered trout and, when it was served, that black porter boned it lickity-split and so expertly that the trout remained totally intact.

When I got to Pueblo I found the big city pretty intimidating. I decided to take a taxi to the arranged meeting place even though it seemed extremely expensive. When I first met Aunt Charlotte she seemed cold and unfriendly. Her manner was abrupt and business-like and she didn't greet me with a warm smile. After I got to know her though she seemed quite nice. She was impressed that I had managed to make the trip by myself without getting lost and that I got to the appointment on time.

Aunt Charlotte introduced me to E.G. Middlekamp, head of the firm that handled my father's estate. From that time, and for the next thirty years or so, I dealt with the Middlekamp Agency, first with the father, E.G. and when he died, with Bob Middlekamp, the son. Most of our business was done by correspondence but on a few occasions I had to make other trips to Pueblo.

The Middlekamp Agency had established a bank account for my father's funds. Each month I wrote a check on that account which I sent to the State Hospital to cover my father's upkeep. My father was given about $5.00 from that check for personal spending money each month. I conscientiously sent my father his funds every month for as long as he lived.

My job as conservatrix finally ended in the early 1960's when my father passed away in the State Mental Hospital at the age of 76. LeRoy accompanied me to Pueblo where we arranged for my father's burial.

Mary and I inherited the remainder of the estate which consisted of bonds in Southern Colorado Power Company and Northern States Power and Light Co. We sold the bonds for about $20,000. Nora's diamond was part of the estate and Mary really wanted it for her daughter, Sydney, so I took the appraised value in cash.

Later when I had time to look through my father's personal belongings which the hospital had turned over to me, I found several diaries that gave me some insight into my father's personality and his life in the hospital. I discovered that he had gone to the World's Fair in St. Louis, that he corresponded with several friends over the years, and that he frequently went shopping in the town of Pueblo.

Along with diaries there were several account books. I was fascinated by my father's fixation with numbers. He recorded every single expenditure from a tube of toothpaste to a new watch and kept a running total of every penny of his money.

THE DRIVING LESSON

Mary: Charles and I were about fourteen when I had my first driving lesson. One Sunday afternoon Charles had his dad's new Essex car and we were driving around picking up a few friends when Charles asked me if I would like to learn to drive. I scooted under the steering

wheel. I could just barely see through the wheel to see the road but we were getting along pretty good when he said, "You can go faster than this, you're doing fine." He put his foot on top of my foot on the gas pedal and down the cemetery road we went. It was a straight road and we were going along at a pretty good clip. Suddenly the road made a sharp left turn but I went straight ahead, up we went over the bank and tipped over. No one was hurt but I was very upset. I cried all the way home. Charles said if he had some reason for the accident his dad would understand so he punctured one of the tires to make it look like that was the cause of the accident. It was a long time until I was willing to have another lesson driving but he did teach me to drive. He was a real good driver himself.

SCHOOL BEHAVIOR

Mary: School discipline was pretty much up to the teacher in those days. I started school in Aspen in the seventh grade. Charles was in the seventh grade too. The seventh and eighth grade students were in the same room and there were two teachers, each of them taking part of the class. The teachers were Nan B. Scales and Alma Short.

One day Charles's teacher, Mrs. Short, said to him, "I expect you to stay after school and finish your English assignment." He said, "I can't stay after school, I have to help sweep my dad's store." She said, " I expect you to stay." He mumbled to himself loud enough for her to hear, "We'll see about that." She went right down the aisle and jerked him by the shoulders to get him out of his seat but his feet were stuck in the cross bars under the desk. She gave another jerk and this time pulled off some of the buttons from his shirt. She dragged him down the aisle toward the door. The door was partly open and, as she pushed it further open, it swung back and hit her in the head. This made her madder than ever. With a yank, she had him out in the hall and, with another push, down the stairs he fell to the first landing. Mrs. Short said, "Now you stay there." and he stayed.

Charles Evans, High School

Mary Evans, High School

ASPEN BASKETBALL TEAM

Mary: Aspen school was pretty small in the early 1930's. There were about thirty five enrolled in the whole high school but almost everyone participated in all the sports and activities. Our boys basketball team was especially good. At that time, teams in the state were not broken up into A and B teams but they played all the other schools, large and small. The year we were seniors in 1932 Aspen beat all the teams on the Western Slope and went to Denver to the championships. They didn't win but we were very proud of them.

Aspen Basketball Team, First Place on Western Slope
Back Row: Freddie Hart, Chester Short, Charles Evans, Reinhard Elder, James Beck, Coach Paul Smith, Edward Stitzer, Johnny Krizman
Front Row: Ewald Crosbey, Roy Hansen, Marshall LaVey, Albert Bishop, _____

CAMPING

Martha: We told about the fact that when we were growing up we went camping a lot to Kelly Lake. Well, after Arbaney bought that property he drained the lake and planted potatoes. We couldn't go

Mom camping up at the Park in 1931.

to Kelly Lake anymore but we continued to go camping for our vacations. There weren't a lot of other things you could do. Chris Hyrup told us that any time we wanted to we could camp at the Park. One time we were camping up at Last Chance, which is a little above where Chris lived and Mary and I went out and we shot a ground hog. Daddy had taught all us kids to shoot the 22 rifle he had. It was an old Stevens. Anyway, we shot a ground hog, skinned it and took it to the camp. We told the rest of the gang that it was a rabbit. Well, of course, we didn't fool Mom but she went along with it. We cooked it and, actually, it wasn't bad.

After we moved to Aspen and Mom was in the telephone office, we still went camping during her vacations. Once we went up to Thomas Lake above Dinkle Lake. Mom let us take friends and, I remember, I took Dorothy Ware. She and I carried our phonograph. It

Tom & Martin John up at the Park on Chris' hay stacker horse.

was a manual cranking table model. It was pretty heavy. We thought it was worth it though as we enjoyed the music every night around the camp-fire. We caught frogs and had fried frog legs while we listened to the music. We built a raft so we could get out to deeper water where the fish were. We caught a lot of fish from the raft. Luckily nobody fell in because not a one of us could swim.

Another time we camped up Independence

Virginia and her friend, Mary Dansdill, up Last Chance.

just below Lost Man in a cabin called Tag Inn. It belonged to a man called Taggert . Later he moved it down to Taggert's Lake. LeRoy, my future husband, went with us that time.

On one of our outings we hiked into Conundrum Hot Springs. Again, each one of us took friends. Tom took Martin John Bishop and Jesse Maddalone. Virginia took Ray, they were going together at the time, Mary took Charles and I took LeRoy. And Mom took us all. It was quite a hike. When we were there we went in the hot springs every

Camping up Conundrum. L to R: Virginia & Ray, Tom & Cubbie, Mary & Charles, Mom, Jesse Maddalone, Martin John Bishop, Martha & LeRoy.

Camping up at the Park in 1931
Front Row Seated: Mary Dansdill, Hazel Hyrup with Bob, Chris Hyrup, Mary
Back Row: Martin John Bishop, Annabelle Hyrup, Gene Hyrup, Mom, Virginia & Tom

day. George Anis ran sheep up in that area. We invited him down to our camp and we played Demon. (Demon is a card game played like multiple solitaire and you must be very quick to win.) George was so funny. Whenever he wasn't playing many off of his Demon pile, he would say, "Oh my Demons, oh my Demons!" After he'd been to visit us, he decided that he would cook us a lamb. So he dug a pit and he cooked it for several hours. Talk about good, it was great! We were there about a week. On our way home we stopped at the rock slide and picked raspberries. We must have gotten a couple of gallons.

Virginia and Cubbie up
Last Chance in 1931

THE SUBSTITUTE TEACHER

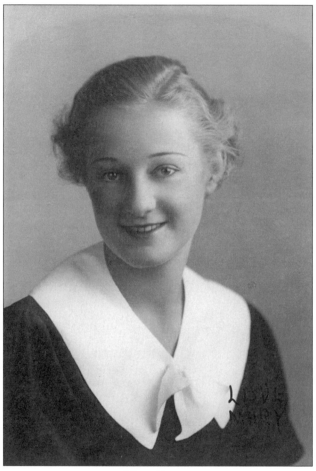

Mary Evans

Mary: Before I went back to school one year, in fact, it was my last year in college, one of the rural schools didn't have a teacher because she had to have an operation. It would be a little over a month until she could come back to school so the school board gave me the job. We walked about two miles to this rural school There were seven children in all the classes together. One family had four children who came galloping up to the school house on their horses with their lard pail lunch boxes filled with cold pancakes. They were so pleased because they had new coveralls and they wanted to show them to me. They were a nice little group of children but the oldest daughter, Christine, was always a little bit afraid of new situations.

One day they heard their mother galloping up to school on her horse. Christine came up to my desk, she was just shaking, and she said, "Don't let her take little Louie." About that time their mother got to the door. I told Christine that I'd do my best. Their mother said she wanted to take the children away before school was out. I said, "If you don't mind waiting a little while we'll be through and they won't have any work to make up." She said she had to go to the post office but she'd be back. I was a little trembly myself because there she was with a gun belt on and a gun in the holster and she looked rather disturbed. As soon as she was well out of sight and going in the other direction, I let the four children go home. Later, when I was back at college, I heard that she had separated from her husband. She had gone with the husband's brother and had taken all the children. They were having a lot of family trouble but I heard later they were doing all right.

LeRoy Waterman 1929, Movie Star Picture

Martha: I think I mentioned a while back that I had visited quite a bit up on the Frying Pan with my friend Virginia Crowley. After we moved to Aspen, she called me one day and said that she had a fella that she kinda liked that was living with them. His name was Clark Waterman. He was working on the road with her dad. Clark's brother, LeRoy, was planning to come for a visit and when he got there she wanted me to come up and meet him. When he arrived she gave me a call. I went up to Virginia's and that's where I met LeRoy. The four of us had quite a bit of fun together. We fished, we hiked and we went on picnics. LeRoy had a car and we went to dances up and down the valley. I went with him all that summer. That fall was the year I started to college. It was 1929, the year of the stock market crash. I didn't see LeRoy during my college years except for a short visit each summer but we did write often. I did have the picture that he gave me when I first met him. I thought he looked like a movie star. I took that picture with me when I went to college and showed it to all the girls in the dorm. They all said, "Oh, he's gorgeous!"

Virginia Crowley. She later married
LeRoy's brother, Clark.

LeRoy, early spring 1932   Martha, early spring 1932

The year I graduated from college, 1933, LeRoy got a job working up at the Twin Lakes Tunnel. He lived at the Hotel Jerome. Believe it or not, in those days, he rented a room at the Hotel Jerome and it cost him five dollars a week. Of course he ate up at the tunnel. That's where most of the men ate. They had a dining room up there. It was during the summer of 1933 that we got engaged.

OUR FAMILY TRIP TO THE WORLD'S FAIR

Mary: As I remember, the second year of the world's fair was in 1934. The Glenwood Post had a contest to sell subscriptions to the Post including unpaid and renewal of the paper. The winner was to receive a trip to the fair on the train from Glenwood Springs, Colorado to Chicago. Sis and I thought it would be great to enter the contest but we wanted our whole family to go, so we asked if we could have the amount of money they were going to allow in cash. The sponsors agreed to do that.

When we first got excited about the Glenwood Post contest, Sis was going with LeRoy and he offered to let us take his car so the whole family could go. We started forging full steam ahead on the project. We never let a day go by without getting around town and all the nearby country to try to sell subscriptions. About every week they posted the progress of the contestants and it was back and forth between a couple in Glenwood Springs and Sis and me. Along near the closing deadline of the contest, LeRoy had the bright idea of our going up to Lincoln Gulch tunnel to sell subscriptions to the men working on the tunnel, a big project to divert water from the Western slope of Colorado to the Eastern slope. LeRoy was working up there and he knew just when the men had pay day. We dressed up a bit and put on our best smiles and arrived just at the right time for them to have money in their pockets. Probably none of them really wanted the local news but they couldn't refuse helping us win a trip to Chicago. In two days the contest ended and we won.

We had been talking about the World's Fair night and day and now we could make definite plans. We decided we should each have some of the responsibilities. Mom had traveled back and forth from Newark, Ohio to Colorado several times on the train but she had never driven a car in her life. Her job was to help with the directions. She had the map and was to watch for road signs to help keep us on the best route. At the time there was no such thing as a driver's license or age limits to drive an automobile. Sis, Tom, Virginia and I were to be the drivers. On my first turn at driving, I nearly hit a bridge abutment so I was taken off the list of drivers and put in charge of the money. When Virginia took her turn she ran up on a curb and we thought the car would tip over so she lost her driving privileges. That left just Sis and Tom to do the driving and they handled it fine.

We took a picnic basket with essentials like peanut butter, a coffeepot and bare necessities for cooking. Tom and Virginia were to help unload and load the car and check to make sure nothing was left behind when we packed up again. I watched the billboards for food specials so we wouldn't spend too much on food. It was fun for all of us to watch the billboards because at that time there were Burma Shave signs every few miles. The signs had funny rhymes on them.

Some friend that had been to Chicago had told us we could find economical lodgings at Oak Park. As we neared the city of Chicago, we could hardly believe the multiple traffic lanes and the cars whizzing by us so fast. Sis said, " If we ever get there, I am going to park this car and we will go any place we go on the "L"." We found Oak Park was not a picnic area, but homes of wealthy people that were still battling the depression. The first place we stopped to inquire about a room was a three-story, beautiful old home. The owner said we could have the whole second floor for five dollars a day for the week we planned to stay. We each had our own room and bath. Everything we needed was included, we could hardly believe our good fortune. We even had a garage for the car. We quickly settled in and fixed a bite to eat.

Our family trip to the World's Fair 1934.
L to R: Tom, Mom, Martha, Virginia
(Picture taken by Mary)

It was about 11:00 P.M. when Mom said, "Let's don't waste our time, we might just as well go out to the fairgrounds and get our bearings for tomorrow." The lady had told us we were just a block away from where we got on the "L" so we went that direction. We had gone a very little way when we saw a YMCA still open, we went in to get information. The man in charge said he was just getting ready to lock up but he would take us as far as he was going and explain where to change. He wrote out good directions and gave us maps and a telephone number to call if we needed any assistance. We figured the good Lord was looking out for us again.

We arrived at the main gate shortly before closing time which was 12:00. Since it was so late the ticket seller said we could go in free and be back at the gate by 12:00. We only had time to look around a little bit and check the layout of the fair. We didn't encounter any problems getting home.

On our first big day at the fair, we used the main entrance as our landmark. Tom and I headed for Modern Transportation and Houses of the Future. As we went I made note of where we could get free food samples. We had agreed to meet at 11:30 for our first lunch which was hot dogs and ice cream - no cost.

One day Mom and I had been looking at various exhibits when she needed a place to rest, no benches were in sight. She said, " Just let me sit on the curb and put my feet in the gutter." She really was tired. She usually got very little exercise because as manager of the telephone office she had to remain near the switchboard 24 hours a day.

One day we all went together to visit the planetarium. It was a permanent building. We had none of us had that type of experience before and we were quite impressed. Another time we each went our own way and agreed to meet at about 7:00 in the evening at the place where they had the fireworks. We didn't dream it would be such a busy place and such a big area crowded with thousands of people but, luck was with us again, and we got together without a problem.

All too soon our vacation time ended and we started home. We came to a detour and drove quite a ways into Wyoming before we got back on the right route. I was still in charge of the food and general expenses. Everyone thought I could have allowed us a little more to eat because we did get home with thirty-seven dollars!

FIRST TEACHING EXPERIENCES

Lower Capital School 1933.
L to R, Back Row: ____, Ray (Bubby) Light, ____, Ruth Lawrence.
Second Row: Mabel Hatch, Mardell Lawrence, Christine Kay, ____.
Front Row: ____, ____, George Kay, Louis Kay, Gertrude Kay

Martha: I had my degree and I had my teaching certificate and all I needed now was a job. I was qualified to teach English, History and Foreign Language but I had no luck finding a high school position. About the middle of the summer I heard about an opening in a one-room school up Old Snowmass for grades 1-8. I applied for that job and got it. The wages were $85 a month, year round. I lived with the Leo Light family for $25 a month board and room. They also provided me with a horse to ride. It was about three miles to the school down through the fields. Not only did I teach but I also did the janitor work. I would get to school in the morning and the first thing I would do was build the fire in the pot-bellied stove. Then I would sweep the floor ... having put sweeping compound on it the night before. The first kids to arrive would bring a bucket of water from the creek. This was our drinking water. There was a dipper in the bucket and I told the kids many times not to drink out of the dipper but use it to fill their cups. Often they forgot and drank from the dipper but none of us ever got sick. When it was time to start school the very first day I was missing four children. I asked the other kids, "Who's not here?" They all said, "The Kays." Just then we looked up the road and we saw, in the distance, a cloud of dust. Four horses came galloping down the road, each with a tow-headed kid riding bareback. The kids pulled their horses to an abrupt stop in front of the school. The oldest child was Christine Kay who was in the sixth grade. Next was George who was in fourth. Gertrude was in second grade and Little Louie was in first. They were all dressed alike in blue and white striped coveralls and they were really cute with their big brown eyes and white hair. I only realized later that the Kay kids wore nothing under their coveralls. One day in October, Little Louie came up to me. He unbuttoned the top button of his coveralls and said ," Lookee here!" He proudly showed me the new long underwear he was wearing. I only realized then that the Kay kids had just two outfits: coveralls with nothing under them but a birthday suit and coveralls with long underwear underneath. I had nine or ten kids that year in grades one through six. When I think back about that class I realize now that they were kind of special. They were well behaved and they appreciated everything you did for them. I put everybody together in one group for Social Studies. I was surprised to find out how much the young ones remembered. I was required to teach the course of study provided by the county superintendent. She came at the end of the year and tested all the kids and I was very happy to learn that all of my students did well.

Earlier I mentioned that I boarded with the Lights, Leo and Mamie. She was quite a prankster. On April Fools Day we all sat down to breakfast - Mamie, Leo, the hired man, their son Bubby who was one of my sixth graders , and me. Mamie had put a piece of cotton in the hired man's pancake and we all knew about it. The hired man was always a great talker. While he was looking at us and telling one of his tall tales he was sawing away on his pancake. When he finally stopped talking and looked down at his plate to figure out why he couldn't cut his pancake, we all shouted," April Fool!"

During the year of teaching when I lived with the Lights, Mrs. Light was on the school board. When they had the school board

Students at the Rock Creek School 1934.

Rock Creek School as it looks today. Located where BRB cabins are.

election Mrs. Light was defeated and Mrs. Williams was elected. As a result, I wasn't rehired for the next school year because Mrs. Williams wanted to make her own choice of teachers. My bad luck - I was in the wrong camp.

Fortunately I was able to find another job in the area. The school was just up the Crystal River at what is now the BRB cabins. This was a step down for me. I now got only $75 a month instead of $85. This was a very poor district. The school was a one-room log building with chinking that was falling out in many places. I used to say you could throw a cat through it anywhere. I had to walk to school that year. I lived with Bob and Nellie Sewell about two miles down the road. I only had five children in that school so I had plenty of time to do extra projects. Before Lincoln's birthday the kids and I built a large log cabin diorama with the figure of Abraham Lincoln lying in front of the fireplace reading a book. One of the kids made Lincoln's head out of modeling clay. These children were even poorer than my first group. They loved school and I loved to do things for them.

Mrs. Sewell was a great cook. She almost always sent a piece of pie in my lunch. One thing she fixed that I liked was dandelion greens. In the spring she'd go out and dig a dishpan full of young dandelion leaves. She fixed them with bacon, cream, a little vinegar, a little sugar and some salt and pepper. Bob and Nellie and I would eat the whole dishpan of greens in one sitting.

Finally I got a job teaching what I had been trained to teach. It was in a small school outside of Sterling, Colorado. There were only six teachers on the staff, three elementary and three high school. I taught English, History and Spanish and coached girls basketball.

The following summer, after that first year in Sterling, LeRoy and I got married. We lived in Denver that summer and kept our marriage a secret because the school board was against having married teachers. At the end of my second year in Sterling, when they asked me to come back, I told them no because I was going to get married. Little did they know I had already been married for a year.

MY HONEYMOON

Martha: I'll have to tell you about my wedding. We got married in Rifle. We didn't make it public because, as I said before, married teachers were not accepted. Mom and Tom went with us. We went to the preacher's house and were married. We were going to go on our honeymoon, very short, up on Grand Mesa. It was pouring, it was just really wet. Several places we stopped had no vacancies but we finally saw a vacancy sign and the people had two available cabins. Perfect! We'd take both of them. Well, while we were signing up for the cabins, a couple came and they were drenched. They had been out in the rain and they were looking for a place to stay. The owner said that we had just

LeRoy and Martha a short time after we were married.
Near Hallam Lake in Aspen.

taken the last two cabins. Well, you know mom, she couldn't stand that. She said, "Don't you think we could all stay in one cabin and let them have the other one?" One cabin did have two rooms but only a curtain divided them. Well, LeRoy agreed so that's how we spent our honeymoon night with Leroy and I on one side of the curtain and Mom and Tom on the other. But the next morning it was a beautiful day, the sun came out, and actually I would say our honeymoon was very successful.

Martha, Tom and Mom. Grand Mesa, July 8, 1937. (LeRoy took the picture.)

LeRoy and Martha, Grand Mesa. The day after we were married.

THE LONG COURTSHIP

Mary Evans in her wedding dress. It was a royal
blue velveteen with brown fur trim on
pockets and collar.

Mary: I would have to say Charles and I had a long courtship. Our family moved to Aspen when I was in the seventh grade. That year someone had a birthday party and asked us both to go. When the party was over, Charles asked me if he could walk me home. We were the best of friends all through high school and sometimes we talked about getting married when we grew up. The country was going through the Depression during that time and we learned the importance of having a job and living economically. When I finished

college I got a job in the far southeastern corner of the state. We kept letters going back and forth often. Then, in November of 1938, I was home for Thanksgiving and Charles proposed again and I surprised him by saying, "Let's do that, let's get married on Christmas day, the church will be already decorated so it won't be a big job for either of our families." And so that's just what we did!

Charles Evans with dog given to him by
his sister, Jane,
when he was first married.

Mary, summer 1937, in front of the
Methodist Church in Aspen where she
was married the next year.

CASTLE CREEK CABINS

Castle Creek Cabins, July 4, 1944. In the foreground, Judy, 2½ years old.
Note the birdhouse LeRoy made!

Martha: We were married July 7, 1937 and, as I said, we spent the rest of the summer in Denver where we'd rented an apartment. When I went back to my teaching job (still Miss Downer as far as they knew). LeRoy went to Aspen and started building the log cabins for our cabin camp (motel nowadays). The first cabin he built was the service station. We fixed it up to live in back. He built the bath-house cabin just behind the service station. It had a <u>Ladies</u> side and a <u>Mens</u> side and was used by us and all of the cabin guests.

Later, after Judy was born, we were too crowded in the one room behind the service station so we converted Cabin #7, on the other side of the bathhouse, into a bedroom for our family. We now had a <u>three room house</u>, only problem was we had to go outside to get from room to room.

In 1947, we bought the other half of the block across the alley from the cabins. LeRoy built us a large, log house with all the rooms under ONE roof. Bobby told his grandmother, "We have a new house

LeRoy in background. Station completed in 1937.

and I don't even have to go outside to get to the bathroom!"

While LeRoy was building the cabins, I continued to teach. The school where I taught was another one-room school up Owl Creek. While teaching at the Owl Creek School I had as one of my students, Sam Stapleton, who still lives in the area.

Earl Cowling, who lived down on McLain Flats, told LeRoy he had

Castle Creek Cabins
On the left, six original cabins and, to the right, the service station. Behind the service station was the bathhouse and the cabin we used as a bedroom.

the perfect horse for me to ride to school. It was a nice looking buckskin, sturdy and short coupled. LeRoy told him to bring it to town and we'd buy it. Something told LeRoy he should try the horse before I got on him. He got on the horse and TALK ABOUT BUCK. That horse took off bucking across the yard and under the clothesline where he lost LeRoy. Needless to say it was not a horse for me. Our neighbor Charlie Gavin, who lived across the street and was a sheep man, saw the horse and said he could use him in his pack string. He took the horse and put a pack on him which he promptly bucked off. Charlie put the pack back on with a lot more weight including several blocks of sheep salt. Perseverance paid off and he was able to use the horse.

As I said, we had eight cabins plus the bath house and service station which was the front part of the cabin where we lived. Only one of the cabins was a double. Mary and Charles lived in it for awhile. When they got ready to go to the shipyards they had a sale. Chuck always had a lot of clothes. Two suits were for sale, a dark brown and a light grey. A local man who wasn't known for his cleanliness was debating which one to buy. He said to his companion, " I think I'll take the dark one. It will hold more dirt."

WAR YEARS

Martha: In the late thirties there wasn't much work to be had so Ray, Charles and LeRoy all worked at the Climax Molybdenum Mine near Leadville. They all hated it, so as soon as they could get something else, even if it was out of the U.S. they did. When World War II broke out, they found jobs in construction connected with the war effort. Charles and Ray went to Alaska. LeRoy went to Canada. He worked for Bechtel-Price-Callahan on the Canol Project in the Northwest Territory. They built air bases. Later LeRoy was out on Adak in the Aleutian Islands doing the same thing and Charles went to Ecuador on a construction job.

Tom McNeil, 1940.

Our brother, Tom, graduated from high school in the spring of 1938. He worked for LeRoy in the service station that summer. In

Tom receiving the Silver Star.

the fall he entered Barnes Business College in Denver. When he completed the course he accepted a business position in Telluride, Colorado. In 1940 Tom enlisted in the U.S. Marines. When the Japs bombed Pearl Harbor, we were beside ourselves with worry because we knew he was on the U.S.S. California. According to the news, the California had been hit. Mom prayed that no news from Tom was good news. As soon as he could, Tom called Mom to say he was O.K. and would write later, which he did. Tom did come home on leave once right after Pearl Harbor, after that there wasn't much news and any letters he did write were censored. We did hear that Tom was wounded at Tarawa and received the Silver Star. Then in July, 1944, Mom got the terrible news by telegram that Tom was killed in action in the Pacific (Saipan). An article from the Aspen Times dated July 20, 1944 follows.

While the men were working in Canada and Alaska, Mary was in Fruita with Mom. The telephone company had transferred Mom to Fruita. Virginia and her son, Leland, who was almost 3 years old, came to stay with me and she helped take care of the kids. Bob was 2½ and Judy was less than a year old. I was teaching and taking care of the cabins. About the only renters we had were the soldiers from Camp Hale. We used the cabin on the other side of the bathhouse as a bedroom. LeRoy had rigged up a bell so when the kids woke up from their naps they could pull the cord and we would know it was time to get them up. (the original intercom - LeRoy should have been an inventor).

Judy (11 months) and Bob (2½ years old) with Virginia.

When the men came home from Alaska and Canada, Mary and Charles and Virginia and Ray all lived in Grand Junction. LeRoy and I remained in Aspen. We had the Phillips 66 service station and the cabins. Since the cabins were equipped for cooking and there was no place to

Judy and Leland (almost 3 years old).

buy groceries on Saturday and Sunday in Aspen, we put in a few staples. That's how we got started in the grocery business.

The war years were a hard time to start into the grocery business

Bob & Leland, 1942.

423 798 Y

UNITED STATES OF AMERICA
OFFICE OF PRICE ADMINISTRATION

WAR RATION BOOK FOUR

Issued to _Robert L. Waterman_
(Print first, middle, and last names)

Complete address _Aspen_

Colo.

READ BEFORE SIGNING

In accepting this book, I recognize that it remains the property of the United States Government. I will use it only in the manner and for the purposes authorized by the Office of Price Administration.

Void if Altered
(Signature)

It is a criminal offense to violate rationing regulations.
OPA Form R-145   16—35570-1

because we had to deal with ration books. Every member of a family, adults and children, received a war ration book for groceries. Sugar, coffee, meat and butter were all rationed. Every sale of these items was paid for with money and ration stamps. The tiny stamps had to be collected and pasted onto sheets. Each type of stamp had to be handled separately. The stamps were turned over to the wholesaler so we could buy more groceries. It required a lot of extra bookwork!

Gasoline was also rationed. For me, that was the hardest part of the rationing program because some people would ask us to sell them more gas than they had stamps for. It was hard to refuse our neighbors and friends but if we didn't we wouldn't have stamps to turn in and soon we'd have no gas to sell.

After the war our family wasn't as close as it had been but we continued to spend time together on holidays.

ROSY THE RIVETER

Mary: When the US got into World War II, jobs in our area were scarce but we heard there was lots of work out on the west coast. We read in the paper that there was a real need for heavy equipment operators that could also keep the equipment repaired. That's what Charles was good at. There was also a short supply of school teachers. We packed up and moved to Portland, Oregon. This was summer of 1944 when Sydney was 3 years old.

When we got to Portland we heard about a welding class just starting at Swan Island. Swan Island was a major ship building center and men and women were being trained to weld on oil tankers that were being constructed.

Nearby, at VanPort, housing was available and we rented an apartment there.

We found that there was an excellent child care program. The child care facility was planned like a large wheel. The spokes separated each age group and it was furnished according to the size of

All Triplers Better known as three plate welders, this Swan Island Swing shift seven does its welding on the foc's'le deck assembly in background. From left, Leadman G. N. Livdahl, F. L. Blakely, G. H. Lidwell, H. B. Browning, Mary Evans, R u b y Cable and Olive Payne. (Swan Island photo)

that age level. A United States flag was in the center of the area. Next to the flag was a sandy playground. Next was a nice grassy play space. Next was hard top for toys on wheels, followed by a covered area for exercise on rainy days. The outer part of the spoke was closed in. This was a nice light room for indoor activities. The bathroom had low toilets and wash bowls.

The staff always seemed pleasant. A doctor and nurse were available. They gave shots when due if requested. Forms were given for the date and type of shots for parents' records.

Another convenience for parents was daily hot meals. A meal or any part of a meal could be ordered and be ready to take home for the family's dinner that evening. Often a small freshly baked loaf of bread was included.

Since such excellent day care was available for Sydney, Charles and I decided to take the welding class. We had to buy leathers to protect us from hot slag. The main suit was overalls, jacket, hood, long sleeved gloves and goggles. I thought those nice brown suits were great. We also had lace-up leather boots with steel toes. I really enjoyed welding. I found it fun to watch that red hot metal go into place.

Charles and I both passed the test for three-place welders: flat, vertical, and overhead.
Most of the women just did flat work. Charles was put on the crew for welding sea chests which had to be good strong welds. I was small and agile so I was able to weld in tight places. I felt like Rosy the Riveter, being able to do jobs that were harder for most of the crew. We all got to watch when the US Swan Island was christened.

OUR TIME IN ECUADOR

Mary: When the welding job was finished, big equipment operators were still very much in demand. Charles was asked to go to the Galapagos Islands to build runways to use for training pilots. Since he would likely be a long time at that construction site, Sydney and I went with him. Only military crews were allowed on the Galapagos so Sydney and I would stay in Guayaquil. Charles would visit us about once a month.

We found room and board with an English lady, Mrs. McGill. She said she usually didn't take children but Sydney completely won her over. Sydney was also a favorite of the other boarders. Sydney was good at entertaining herself. One day she was sitting on her bed coloring when she dropped her crayon behind the bed. She couldn't get at it so we moved the bed out a little and there was a tarantula. I quickly called Mrs. McGill. She called the houseboy and he and the other boarders came running with brooms and swatters. They soon got the tarantula.

An American teacher had a school called Colegio Americano. I was asked to teach a 4th grade reading class in English. All morning classes were in English and afternoon classes were in Spanish. Sydney was enrolled in kindergarten. She often said, "We talk to each other but we don't know what the other one says." With my English-Spanish dictionary we managed to get to school and back on the bus.

The runway construction and the school term ended and we moved back to Colorado. Fruita Elementary needed a third grade teacher and I took the job. Sydney was just ready to start first grade. Charles was asked to continue working on landing fields in Panama. We were all busy again.

Into Each Life
a Little Rain Must Fall

A Tribute to the Deceased

Thomas Roe McNeil

1919-1944

In July of 1944, mom got the terrible news, by telegram, that Tom was killed in action in the Pacific. An article from the Aspen Times dated July 20, 1944 follows:

Aspen Times

ASPEN, COLORADO   Thursday July 20, 1944   EVERY FRIDAY MORNING

Sgt. Thos. R. McNeil Killed in Action

**WAR IS BROUGHT TRAGICALLY HOME TO ASPEN
AS WELL-KNOWN HOME BOY IS KILLED IN
SERVICE OF HIS COUNTRY**

Platoon Sergeant Thomas R. McNeil, 25, son of Mrs. Faith McNeil of Aspen and Fruita, was killed in action in the Pacific, Mrs. McNeil was informed in a telegram from Lt. Gen. A. A. Vanrergrif,, Commandant of the Marine Corps, Wednesday morning. Mrs. McNeil is in Aspen at the home of her daughter, Mrs. LeRoy C. Waterman.

USMC Photo Showing Sergeant McNeil Being Decorated for Gallantry in Action at Tarawa

The telegram, which gave only brief details, follows:

Mrs. Faith R. McNeil, Fruita, Colo.

Deeply regret to inform you that your son, Platoon Sergeant Thomas R. McNeil, USMC, was killed in action in the performance of his duty and in service to his country. No information is available at present regarding disposition of remains. Temporary burial in locality where death occurred, probably. You will be promptly furnished any additional information received. To prevent possible aid to our enemies, do not divulge name of his ship or station. Please accept my heartfelt sympathy. Letter follows.

A. A. VANDEDGRIF, LT. GEN., USMC

Thomas R. McNeil was born in Basalt, on February 23rd, 1919. He attended the Basalt grade schools and Aspen High school, where he graduated. Following graduation he went to Denver, where he attended business college, later accepting a business position at Telluride.

In 1940, at virtually the first call to arms of his country, he enlisted in the United States Marines, the heroic fighting outfit which has distinguished itself in every conflict in this nation's history. He took his training at San Diego and was later assigned to duty on the U. S. S. California.

He was serving on the California when the japs struck at Pearl Harbor. He was with the first units to land at Tarawa and in that terrific battle he was injured, but despite his wounds he stayed with his men until the situation was secure before he would permit himself to be treated by medical corpsmen.

For gallantry in action on that occasion he was awarded the Silver Star, a rare and highly treasured decoration. Further, he received the Purple Heart. When details are finally known he will undoubtedly receive an additional citation for making the supreme sacrifice for his country.

Sergeant McNeil is survived by his mother, Mrs. Faith R. McNeil, four sisters, Mrs. LeRoy C. Waterman of Aspen; Mrs. Charles Evans, Portland, Oregon; Mrs. Ray Hendricks, Aspen; and Mrs. Alfred Hyrup of Los Angeles.

Virginia Downer Hendricks
1917-1958

Our sister, Virginia, was an excellent music teacher, loved by her students and the members of the community. She was a thoughtful and loving mother. She started married life being able to cook only bean salad and cocoa, but through practice became a very good cook. Virginia died after a battle with cancer in 1958 when she was only 41 years old.

Faith Roe McNeil
1887-1968

Our mother, Faith McNeil, was always an inspiration to all of the family. Besides working and raising our family she was very active in civic affairs. Mom started the Fruita, Colorado Thrift Shop to help raise money to build a new hospital. A friend, Ada Mecham, once said that if there was ever a "perfect lady" it was our mother. In 1968 she was given the Ruth B. Wyper Award for civic service. She remained active and alert until her death in 1968 at the age of 81.

Ray Irving Hendricks
1914-1973

Virginia's husband, Ray, lived in Basalt and drove to Aspen to work every day for years. In fact, he received an award for being such a safe driver. In the winter of 1973 there was a lot of snow. Ray was driving the Buttermilk bus and he had to get out and shovel snow. it was too strenuous for him and he had a fatal heart attack. He was only 59 years old when he died.

Thomas Charles Evans
1949-1978

Mary's son, Tom, was an avid kayaker. On June 10th of 1978 he and his cousin Ken planned to spend the day on the Eagle River up toward Vail. The water was very turbulent and Tom's kayak turned over and he was unable to right it. Ken did everything he could but to no avail. Mary and Charles received the news later that day that Tom had drowned in the accident. Their only consolation was that Tom had died doing what he loved to do. He was 29 years old when he died.

LeRoy C. Waterman
1907-1985

Martha's husband, LeRoy, was according to her the best husband and father that she could ever have wanted. He worked hard all of his life, but he also liked to have a good time. He loved to travel and he loved people. When he developed emphysema and had to depend on an oxygen tank, it was something he couldn't tolerate. He took his own life in 1985 at the age of 78.

Charles Morgan Evans
1914-1993

Mary's husband, Charles, was always quite an outdoor person. He often found rocks that reminded him of certain things. He was a great one to tell tales to his grandchildren. One day he found a rock that looked like a skull and he told the grandkids it was one of his ancestors, the great Gera BomBom. When Mary and Charles left Basalt, their granddaughters said they had to take Gera BomBom along. When Charles died in 1993 at the age of 78, the family agreed to use Gera BomBom as his headstone.

Kids, Grandkids, & Great-Grandkids

Our Family as of the Year 2000

MARTHA'S FAMILY

Son, Bob Waterman
Daughter-in-law,
    Gayle Carter Waterman

Daughter, Judy Waterman
Huston
Son-in-law, Nick Huston
Grand-son, Jordan Huston
Golden Retriever, Tex

VIRGINIA'S FAMILY

Daughter, Kathy Hendricks Flynn
and her retriever friends

Grand-daughter, Dana Hertler,
Lou Hertler, her husband, and
Sons, Coty and Brandon Hertler

VIRGINIA'S FAMILY

Son, Leland and
his wife, Jeanne

Front Row: Grand-daughter, Ginnie
Hendricks Swanson, Great-grand-son,
Joseph Swanson
Back Row: Great-grand-daughters,
Suzanne Swanson and Leigh Swanson

Grand-son, Roger Hendricks
his wife, Stacy and
Great-grand-daughter, Sierra

VIRGINIA'S FAMILY

Grand-son, Timothy Hendricks and
his wife, Sarah Hendricks

Grand-daughter, Debra; Daughter-in-law, Jeanne; Grand-son, Michael;
Grand-son, Tony; Grand-daughter, Kim; Grand-daughter, Lisa; Grand-daughter, Anne

Daughter, Sydney Evans Rupar and Mary Evans
picking apples at Pepper Bridge Farm

Son-in-law, Bob Rupar and
Great-grand-son, Peter Warinner

Grand-daughter, Amy Evans Warinner,
her husband, John Warinner, and
Great-grand-children,
Hannah, Peter, and Molly Warinner

Grand-daughter, Denise Evans Shives,
her husband, Tom Shives, and
Great-grand-daughter,
Jessica Shives

Grand-daughter, Natalie Evans Davis and
her husband, Todd Davis

We're Still Here
The Year 2000

We didn't sit in our rocking chairs after we retired. **We kept busy!** We both loved to play bridge and have continued to enjoy the game on into the new Millennium. We had not one but two big gardens! Mary raised the peas and beans in her garden on Willits Lane near El Jebel. Martha planted the potatoes and corn in her garden at Basalt. We both grew raspberries, strawberries and all the other garden vegetables. One year we raised sunflower seeds for the birds.

We both did quite a lot of travelling. The two trips we went on together were special. One trip to England and Scotland we took with our daughters and the other trip was to Venezuela.

The two of us went with the Audubon Society to Venezuela on a bird watching expedition. We still say "Once a bird watcher, always a bird watcher"

Mary and Martha on the Orinoco River in Venezuela toasting a successful day of bird watching and **A WONDERFUL LIFE!**